POWer Strategies™
for Reading Comprehension

Grades 3–5

by
Terry L. Romer, M.A.

Printed in the U.S.A.

Author: Terry L. Romer, M.A.   **Editor:** Jill Campbell Reed   **Page Layout & Graphics:** Adrienne M. Speer

These popular teacher resources and activity books are available from
ECS Learning Systems, Inc.

ECS9676	Destinations	Grades 5–9
ECS2371	Grammar Notebook: Parts of Speech	Grades 9–12
ECS238X	Grammar Notebook: Sentence Structure	Grades 9–12
ECS2398	Grammar Notebook: Punctuation, Capitalization, and Spelling	Grades 9–12
NU783XRH	Graphic Organizer Collection	Grades 3–12
ECS9501	Hemingway for Teachers	Grades 9–12
ECS9609	Inkblots	Grades 6–12
ECS0484	Not More Writing?!	Grades 9–12
ECS9633	Odysseys	Grades 5–9
ECS948X	Quick Thinking	Grades 7–12
ECS9706	Springboards for Reading	Grades 7–12
ECS0549	Structures for Reading, Writing, Thinking Book 1	Grades 4–9
ECS0557	Structures for Reading, Writing, Thinking Book 2	Grades 4–9
ECS0565	Structures for Reading, Writing, Thinking Book 3	Grades 4–9
ECS0573	Structures for Reading, Writing, Thinking Book 4	Grades 4–9
NU5958RH	Tackling Literary Terms	Grades 9–12
ECS9439	Tactics to Tackle Thinking	Grades 7–12
ECS9668	Voyages	Grades 5–9
ECS9080	Writing Warm-Ups	Grades 7–12
ECS9463	Writing Warm-Ups Two	Grades 7–12

To order, or for a complete catalog, write:
ECS Learning Systems, Inc., P.O. Box 440, Bulverde, TX 78163-0440
Web site: **www.educyberstor.com**
1 • 800 • 688 • 3224

ISBN-10: 1-57022-656-3   ISBN-13: 978-1-57022-656-4

POWer Strategies™
for Reading Comprehension

Grades 3–5

by
Terry L. Romer, M.A.

Table of Contents

Preface

"Reading is understanding." How many times I have said that to my reading students over 32 years of teaching! A truly powerful reader at any grade level is one who comprehends the material. From the first grader who suddenly realizes the sounds and words are conveying a message to the high-school student whose reading goes beyond the simple text to evaluation and synthesis of material, comprehension is the goal of all reading.

I have heard teachers at all levels discuss students who read fluently, decode, and "word-call" well, but have no idea what the message of the text might be. I first observed this in English Acquisition students before realizing that it was a common trait in most of my remedial reading students. The idea that reading is for meaning was overshadowed by the importance of "getting the words right." In middle school and high school classes, this is especially significant because students can sound literate in classroom oral reading without comprehending the text. Many content teachers at the upper levels are unaware that a poor reader can sound fluent but still need extra help understanding what they have read.

I previously wrote *POWer Strategies™ for Reading Comprehension* for Grades 6–8 to address comprehension instruction in the middle grades. Teachers who have taken my university class, "Organization and Management of Reading Classrooms," pointed out that the same content should be taught at elementary grades. Their proactive thinking resulted in *POWer Strategies™ for Reading Comprehension* for Grades 3–5. Phonemic awareness, phonics, word attack, and vocabulary work are all essential tools in learning to read. This book focuses on the comprehension skills that are also essential to becoming a powerful reader. It is my hope that teachers who use this book will work on a balanced approach that addresses both word attack and comprehension.

Please use this book as a guide to which you add your own ideas and chart your own course. Every teacher has the ability to teach Power Strategies and influence students to become true power readers.

Terry L. Romer, M.A.

Introduction

POWer Strategies™ for Reading Comprehension provides 28 weeks of suggested lessons, activities, take-home letters, and quizzes. Additionally, there are suggested word-attack skills included each week to review word-attack lessons from previous grades. These suggestions can be adjusted to any teacher's philosophy or schedule.

This book consists of:
1. **Detailed daily lesson plans** for the first week of the school year.
2. **Lessons for weeks 2–28** which can be taught as "mini-lessons" while working with the stated skills/strategies in class novels. Twenty-eight weeks of plans allows for extra time for testing days, assemblies, field trips, and other activities during the year. Additionally, teachers may prefer to expand lessons to include word attack and vocabulary as necessary.
3. **Activities** to accompany all skills and strategies.
4. **Quizzes** to assess student progress in each weekly topic. Each quiz can be found following the last activity for each section.
5. **Weekly take-home letters** to inform parents/guardians and to use as a log of reading completed at home. Take-home sheets are designated with a 🏠. Be sure to collect the reading logs each Friday. Rewards can be given for any reading done at home.
6. An **index of suggested novels** for group work for grades 3–5.
7. A **list of "read alouds"** for the teacher to use in class.
8. An **appendix of "bell-starter" activities.**

Week 1—Setting Up for Success

Many activities in *POWer Strategies*™ *for Reading Comprehension* include cooperative group work. A class community with well-defined standards, rules, and expectations will make greater strides throughout the school year. Plans for Week 1 address these issues.

Day 1

1. Assign seats on the first day of school. Returning students often know many of their classmates and have determined where they would like to sit. By mixing up this pre-planned arrangement, teachers can make their own decisions about seating organization. On the first day students can be handed a card at the door to match with a card on a desk or simply be seated alphabetically. The second and third day should follow different patterns until the teacher has a good "handle" on the situation and can make a more permanent seating chart.

As students enter the classroom, they are told to complete the "bell-starter" activity. Appendix II (page 160) includes a list of these activities. This procedure lets the teacher greet each student and take roll as students are engaged in an activity. Take a few minutes to go over responses to the bell-starter after roll is taken.

2. Pair the students and have them talk for three or four minutes each. Ask them to write interesting facts about each other on the cards provided. Then each student introduces his/her partner to the class using the information learned during their talks. Teachers can suggest topics to discuss, such as siblings, interests, and pets. Write down a word or two about each child as this presentation is being given. Transferring these words onto the permanent seating chart will help personalize lessons later in the year.

3. The first day of school should be for introducing rules, procedures, consequences, and rewards. Two important procedures have already been introduced. Students know that they will have a bell-starter each morning when they enter the class. They also know that listening respectfully when others are speaking, as practiced during the introductions of each other, is a classroom expectation.

Having a rules chart on the wall can be very important. Each class has its own particular needs. A simple chart with no more than five rules should be sufficient. Discuss why "Be kind. Be safe. Be a learner." incorporates all instances of behavior in the classroom. Have students give examples of what each rule means.

Consequences and rewards should be in place on the first day of school. Elementary students enjoy knowing that their good behavior will be rewarded. Explaining systems for rewards and consequences on the first day of school and reviewing them daily for the first week can prevent future problems.

4. Students should complete Figure #1-1, Find-a-Friend Activity, on page 10. Using a copy of this matrix, students will find that they have many things in common with their classmates. After the students have finished the activity, discuss which boxes were difficult to fill and which were easier. This can be a time of enjoyment as students learn about each other and have a chance to move around.

5. This is an excellent time to settle into a read-aloud session. Explain to the children that you will be reading to them every day, as time permits. A list of suggested books for read-aloud time can be found in Appendix I on page 159. This is a quiet time, with students either sitting and listening or drawing pictures of what they are visualizing as you read (see Week 7—Visualization and Imagery). The first day is a good time to introduce a novel, ending your reading with a "cliffhanger" to make students want to hear more the next day.

6. Allowing students time to tour the classroom is another "get out of your seat" activity for the first day of school. Figure #1-2 is a sheet students can complete as they explore the classroom. Each student will be expected to find areas, equipment, materials, and books they will need to use during the year. By searching for these, they will retain the information longer than if the teacher simply points out what they need to know. The students feel like explorers and are ready and willing to use their new knowledge about their classroom.

7. Give students a reason to want to return to class the next day. Ask them to bring in a picture (photo, postcard, brochure, hand-drawn picture) of what they did over the summer. Ask them what they think will happen in the class read-aloud novel. Talk about the rewards for good behavior that will be distributed the second day.

Note: Obviously, much more will be happening on the first day. These plans set the basis for beginning positive procedures and instruction in reading. Use these plans only as they correspond to school or district requirements for classes and other subjects being taught.

Day 2

1. While the teacher greets students at the door, students go directly to their seats and begin the bell-starter. They continue working until roll is taken and the teacher starts the discussion of the bell-starter.

2. Quickly review rules, consequences, and rewards that were discussed yesterday. Let students share instances when they followed procedures and rules.

3. Follow-up on any assignments you might have given at the end of class yesterday. Did students bring a picture or remember what they wanted to know about the novel?

4. The class should discuss the question "What makes a good reader?" Brainstorm this question and write answers on chart paper that can be displayed in the room. Discuss the list, and add and delete ideas. Students in grades 3–5 generally think that good readers always read fast. Explain that they will be learning about times when reading fast is not good. Perhaps the concept could be written, "Good readers adjust their speed when necessary." Make sure to include ideas of your own that are based in good research and practice but written in appropriate language for children.

5. Ask each child to find a book on the bookshelves that looks interesting. They may take the book to their seat and look through it to see if it is a "free reading" book they might like.

6. Many children have never thought about books being important in their lives. Teachers should bring a box of books that have been important in their own lives to share with the class. This technique has been done at all grade levels and is described in Cris Tovani's book *I Read It, But I Don't Get It* (Stenhouse Publishers, 2000). Suggested books teachers might want to share are those they were read from as children, first books they read themselves, books from their travels, books they've read over and over, books by favorite authors, and books they read to their own children.

Students are asked to bring a book(s) to class the next day that is important to them in some way. Figure #1-3 is a form that can be completed by the child and his/her parents/guardians for this purpose. If students do not have the books they wish to present, they may draw a picture of the cover to bring instead of the actual book.

7. Visit the school library. Many librarians or media specialists welcome students the first few days of school to explain rules and procedures and show the materials available.

Day 3

1. After the bell-starter and other routines, review classroom rules and procedures again. Each student can write the rules on a paper to take home to share with parents/guardians. Ask that these rules are read and signed by a parent/guardian, then returned to school. This is an effective way to ensure that there is no question about acceptable behavior later in the year.

2. All students share the books and forms they brought to class. Reinforce the standards of group listening and respect that were taught on the first day of class. As each child finishes his/her presentation, comments from others should be shared. This is the first Book Share of the year and a good opportunity for students to learn that everyone has different tastes in books and that the level of book being shared is not important. What is important is that everyone participates. Book Shares will be a part of *POWer Strategies*™ *for Reading Comprehension* at least monthly throughout the year.

3. Setting a purpose for reading is the topic for next week, but can be touched upon this first week of school. Brainstorm "why we read." We read for enjoyment, safety, information, etc. By keeping their answers on a large chart, material for next week's lessons on setting a purpose for reading is already prepared.

4. After discussing why we read, it is fun to discuss what we read. Again, a large class poster can be made that will be added to throughout the school year. When students realize that their reading is not just in books, but street signs, cereal boxes, medicine, and hundreds of other places, they begin to realize the importance of reading in their everyday lives. Display the poster where students can add to it as they develop their awareness of reading material.

5. **Homework Assignment**—Bring a piece of text (anything that can be read) that is not a book. This assignment makes students aware of the variety of reading material around them.

Day 4

1. After the bell-starter and daily morning routines, ask the students to line up in order by their birthdays (provide a list of the months in order on the board). The only catch to this activity is that they must not speak. It may take a few moments, but eventually someone will hold up three fingers for March or seven for July and others will follow suit. Watching how the group dynamics develop during this activity can show teachers much about leaders, followers, etc.

2. Go over yesterday's homework assignment. Let each child explain the piece of text he/she has brought to class. Are there examples that should be added to the poster of what we read? Ask the students why they think this homework was assigned. Are they aware that reading is important in all aspects of their lives? Ask them to name a job or career in which reading is not necessary. How do their parents/guardians use reading daily? Take a walk around the school building looking for people who are reading and for reading material that is necessary for everyone in the school. Come back to class and discuss what students observed.

3. Ensure that each child has a "free reading" book at his/her desk. Practice reading this book as a time filler when finished with other work, or set a timer for five minutes of reading. Let each child make a bookmark out of tagboard with his/her name and places to write the names of books as they are read. As these bookmarks are filled, they can be posted on a bulletin board and new ones distributed. This makes a great visual display of the reading being done as the year progresses.

4. Remember to read aloud every day. Be sure to stop occasionally while reading and ask questions. Model the kind of questioning you do as a reader.

5. Homework Assignment—Ask each child to ask an adult (parent, older sibling, babysitter, etc.) to tell about their favorite books as a child. Complete Figure #1-4 and present this to the class tomorrow.

Day 5

1. Share the homework assignment from yesterday. Who was interviewed about favorite childhood books? What books were named? Ask the students why this was assigned. Did they discover something about the reading habits of adults in their lives?

2. Administer an Interest Inventory, Figure #1-5. Keep a list of interests with the seating chart by writing an interest by each child's name as a reminder to find materials, make comments, and use students' passions and interests to keep lessons interesting. This is also helpful when ordering materials. A class with several children who are interested in dogs, for instance, will appreciate books, magazines, and other resources about dogs written at appropriate levels.

3. Since classrooms are often well-stocked with books, students can be overwhelmed with choices. Frequent book talks by the teacher will introduce books available and help narrow down the selections for children. Reviewing four or five books of different genres each week gives students a taste of the variety of classroom materials.

4. Day 5 is a good time for students to check out books from the classroom to take home and read. Each teacher has a different way to keep track of books being checked out. Some make a chart on the wall that students sign with the title, date, and their own names. Others have pockets in the books and cards to be filled out and filed alphabetically. The important thing is to have a system and make the procedure automatic for the children.

5. The last day of the week is a good time to look at rewards for weekly behavior and work. A piece of candy, a pencil, or other trinkets are inexpensive, but their impact on students is positive.

Congratulations! The first week is finished, and much has been accomplished. The students know each other and feel that you know them, too. Procedures and rules are in place. Reasons for reading and a survey of materials that are read have been explored. Parents/guardians have been notified of procedures and expectations. Great work!

Find-a-Friend Activity

Directions: Walk around the classroom and find a person who can sign each box. Do not let one person sign more than two boxes.

I have a brother. _____ _____	I can fly a kite. _____ _____	I have milked a cow. _____ _____	I have a sister. _____ _____
My first name starts with a vowel. _____ _____	I have broken a bone. _____ _____	I wear braces. _____ _____	I can ski. _____ _____
I like spinach. _____ _____	I have been to the ocean. _____ _____	My favorite color is blue. _____ _____	I was born in February. _____ _____
I can whistle. _____ _____	I have relatives in another state. _____ _____	I have a cat. _____ _____	I play soccer. _____ _____

Explore Our Classroom

Directions: Write the answer to each question after you find the answer in the classroom.

1. How many desks are there for students? _____

2. Where is lined paper kept? _____

3. Where is the calendar? _____

4. Where is the bell-starter activity found? _____

5. Where are the fire drill directions? _____

6. Is there a telephone in the room? _____

7. How many math books are in the room? _____

8. Where are the science books? _____

9. What is on the teacher's desk? _____

10. Where can students sit on the floor? _____

11. Where do reading groups meet? _____

12. What are the class rules? _____

_____

_____

Important Book Form

Directions: In class we have learned about books that are important in our lives. They might be books we read in school or books that were read to us at home. They might be hard or easy books. Important books have meant something special to us. For homework tonight, find a book that is important to you and complete this form. Then present the book and form in class tomorrow. If you don't have the book to bring, draw the cover on the back of this paper.

Title of book: _____

Author: _____

Reason #1 that this book is important to me: _____

_____

_____

_____

_____

Reason #2 that this book is important to me: _____

_____

_____

_____

_____

Remember to practice reading this form out loud. You will be presenting it to your classmates tomorrow.

Book Interview with an Adult

Directions: Our class wants to know about books important people in our lives read when they were children. Choose one or two adults and ask them to tell about books they enjoyed when they were young.

Name of person I interviewed: _____

Relationship of this person to me: _____

Favorite book(s): _____

_____

What this book was about: _____

_____

_____

Where this book was found (library, etc.): _____

Why was this a special book? _____

_____

_____

_____

Be sure to thank the person you interviewed.

Interest Inventory

1. My favorite TV show is _____.

2. After school I like to _____.

3. On the weekends I like to _____.

4. My favorite book is _____.

5. One thing I do very well is _____.

6. I would like to read a book about _____.

7. Someday I would like to be a _____.

8. My favorite sport is _____.

9. If I could go anywhere, it would be to _____.

10. What I wish I could do better is _____.

11. My best friend is _____.

12. An adventure I'd like to have is _____.

13. My favorite movie is _____.

Name: _____

Figure #1-6

Reading Connection Newsletter

Dear Parents/Guardians:

   You will be receiving this Reading Connection letter every Friday. In it you will be told what we are learning and what can be done at home to help your child be a successful reader. At the bottom of each letter is a tear-off form for you to fill out as your child reads at home. Daily reading outside of school is a major indicator of reading success. Do not feel that every day on the sheet must be filled out. Only mark the days your child actually reads. Rewards will be given when students return this form on Friday mornings.

   This week we learned about reasons for reading and what kinds of materials are read. As you have seen from the homework, we are learning about the importance of reading in daily life. Thank you for setting a reading example at home and showing your child that reading is important to you.

   Next week we will be learning to set a purpose for reading, which is an important concept in literacy. Be sure to ask your child to explain what he/she is learning as the week progresses.

   Thank you for your help and support. Please be sure to return the bottom of this form next Friday morning.

- -

Please write the date next to each day.

Friday _____ Minutes read _____	Saturday _____ Minutes read _____	Sunday _____ Minutes read _____	Monday _____ Minutes read _____
Tuesday _____ Minutes read _____	Wednesday _____ Minutes read _____	Thursday _____ Minutes read _____	

Student's name _____

Parent/Guardian signature _____ Date _____

Week 2—Setting a Purpose for Reading

Setting a purpose for reading gives a direction and focus to reading. It takes very little time to set a reason and can be done by the student or by a teacher. Sometimes the purpose is set by questions in the text itself. Readers simply ask themselves questions such as "What animals will I learn about that live in the Amazon jungles?" or "How will the main character solve the problem I read about yesterday?" The purpose for reading is answering the question. Teachers can use this technique before any reading in class to direct students to focus on why they are reading. When reading aloud to the class, the teacher can model this strategy by asking questions to be answered during that session. Homework assignments can be recorded on a form that actually states "My question to answer while doing this assignment is
_____" or "By reading this, I will learn _____."

Frequently, students say, "I don't understand this," after reading assigned work or individually chosen material. Answering with "What were you looking for when you read?" will reinforce the idea that a reason must have been set in order for the material to make sense. Individual reading logs in class can be developed with the statement, "My purpose for reading this today is _____" as a reminder to always set a purpose before beginning.

One of the most effective ways of setting a purpose is to preview the text to be read. In doing this, students can begin to develop questions to be answered and establish a purpose for reading.

Lessons and Activities

1. After discussing setting a purpose, take the students for two walks around the school building. Before the first walk, set no purpose. Simply go for a stroll. Before the second walk, set a purpose such as "We are going to count the number of posters in the hallway." After returning from the second walk, discuss the difference between the two walks. Ask about the reasons for the walks, and talk as a group about the learning that took place each time.

2. Distribute a reprinted newspaper article or short story to the children. Have them read it without a purpose, then with a purpose. Compare what they got out of the article each time. Was it easier to understand what they read the second time?

3. Using a novel he/she has not read, each student previews the text and answers the questions on Figure #2-1. This provides practice in previewing and establishing a purpose, as well as developing questions to be answered.

4. Provide several genres of text. Ask students to each choose a text (book, newspaper, Internet reprint, comic, magazine, etc.). Each student should preview the material and share in small groups what purpose each would set for reading and what questions he or she would want to answer.

5. Display and discuss last week's chart outlining reasons for reading. Students should complete Figure #2-2. On this activity, they are given several types of text and asked to suggest a purpose for reading each type. Point out that there might be more than one correct response for each text. One person might read the newspaper for entertainment, another for information.

6. **Homework Assignment**—Bring one piece of text from home and describe a purpose for reading it.

Setting a Purpose for Reading and Previewing Material

Directions: Using a novel or class book you haven't read, preview the text and answer these questions.

1. What do the front and back covers tell me about this book? _____

   _____

   _____

2. Does the size of the print tell me that the book will be easy or hard to read?

   _____

3. How many pages are in this book? _____

4. Are there pictures in the book? What do they show? _____

   _____

   _____

5. Is there a table of contents, an index, or other things that will make reading this book easier?

   _____

   _____

6. Does this look like a book I would enjoy reading? _____

7. What is my purpose for reading this text? _____

   _____

8. What questions do I have after looking at this book that I will have to answer as I read?

   _____

   _____

   _____

   _____

Setting a Purpose for Reading

Directions: List a purpose for reading each type of text.

Text	Why I might read this
1. Novel	_____
2. Math textbook	_____
3. Magazine	_____
4. Internet site	_____
5. Newspaper	_____
6. Science book	_____
7. The side of a cereal box	_____
8. Medicine bottle	_____
9. Menu	_____
10. Game directions	_____
11. Bumper stickers	_____
12. Comic book	_____
13. Map	_____
14. TV Guide	_____
15. Social studies book	_____

Quiz—Setting a Purpose for Reading

1. What does it mean to set a purpose for reading?

_____

_____

_____

2. Why should we always set a purpose for reading?

_____

_____

_____

3. Give an example of a text and a reason for reading it.

_____

_____

_____

4. What is previewing text?

_____

_____

_____

5. What can you learn by previewing text?

_____

_____

_____

Name: _____

Figure #2-4

Reading Connection Newsletter

Dear Parents/Guardians:

This week we have learned about setting a purpose for reading. We have discussed and practiced using this technique to give direction and focus to our reading. We also learned about previewing text (anything that can be read). Looking over what we are going to read prepares us for reading and gives us questions to be answered as we read. Please ask your child to describe setting a purpose for reading and to give you an example of this strategy.

Next week we will be talking about using background knowledge to help us understand what we read. We must link our reading to something we already know. Connecting our prior knowledge to our present reading makes it relevant and easier to comprehend.

Below is this week's reading log to be filled out at home, signed, and returned on Friday morning. Please remember what an important part of learning daily reading is. Good soccer players must practice. Good musicians must practice. Good readers must practice.

Please write the date next to each day.

Friday _____	Saturday _____	Sunday _____	Monday _____
Minutes read	Minutes read	Minutes read	Minutes read
_____	_____	_____	_____
Tuesday _____	Wednesday _____	Thursday _____	
Minutes read	Minutes read	Minutes read	
_____	_____	_____	

Student's name _____

Parent/Guardian signature _____ Date _____

Week 3—Background Knowledge

All good readers must activate their background knowledge to comprehend reading material. Adults often have vast experiences in learning about the world which translate into schema, or background knowledge. Adults automatically refer to this prior knowledge when making sense of printed text. Having been to Florida, read about Florida, or talked to people from Florida provides a basis of knowledge that can be activated when reading about hurricanes in that region. Children have a smaller base of prior knowledge, but need to refer to their schema to comprehend what they are reading. A student who has no knowledge of glaciers is not able to understand the sentence, "The ship passed a glacier." To that student, a glacier might be another ship, an island, or a type of whale. Teachers have the responsibility to determine that necessary background knowledge is in place before assigning work. This is accomplished through questioning, vocabulary strategies, class discussions, cooperative learning strategies, and careful observation of students.

Students make three types of connections, or links, to the text they are reading. These are text-to-self, text-to-text, and text-to-world. Many teachers use these connections constantly to remind children to activate their background knowledge. Text-to-self connections are used by asking, "What does this remind me of in my own life? Is this something that makes me think of myself, my family, or my friends?" A child who has been to Florida will read about hurricanes and remember being on a beach similar to the one he is reading about. Text-to-text connections remind readers of something they have read previously or a TV show or movie they have seen. Remember, television and movie scripts are text, as are song lyrics and poems. If a student read a book about hurricanes, he/she can relate to the current text about Florida's weather. Text-to-world connections make readers search their schema for news reports and other information they have seen or heard about the world around them. A child might remember hearing someone describe what it was like to be in a hurricane. This information was stored in the child's prior knowledge to be referred to when the word "hurricane" is brought up.

> *Text-to-self connections are used by asking, "What does this remind me of in my own life? Is this something that makes me think of myself, my family, or my friends?"*
>
> *Text-to-text connections remind readers of something they have read previously or a TV show or movie they have seen.*
>
> *Text-to-world connections make readers search their schema for news reports and other information they have seen or heard about the world around them.*

By connecting what is already known to what is being read, students find that material becomes easier to comprehend. In fact, without background knowledge, very little comprehension can take place.

Lessons and Activities

1. Discuss the three text connections (text-to-self, text-to-text, and text-to-world). Using Figure #3-1, ask students to read the passage and write three text connections they made as they read.

2. Read *The Stinky Cheese Man* by Jon Scieszka, or another picture book. As students make text connections with the book, write them on the board under the headings T-to-S, T-to-T, and T-to-W. Discuss how many are in each category. Why is it easier to make a text-to-self connection than a text-to-world? What words in the text were key to making connections?

3. Conduct a class discussion about strategies readers use when reading. Make a wall chart of these to which other strategies will be added during the year. Students may not be aware of all the good strategies they are already using until they see them on the chart. Be sure to include making text connections, setting a purpose, drawing on background knowledge, and previewing material, as these are techniques already learned in class.

4. Using the Strategies Good Readers Use wall chart (#3 above), ask students to read a common piece of text. A reprint of a fairy tale or a newspaper article would be a good choice of material. During reading, each child will write in the margins as they use a good strategy. Repeating this activity during the year will reinforce the use of the chart as a way of improving comprehension. Wall posters such as these are "works in progress" and reflect the learning being done in class. They are also excellent references for students if they need assistance or reminders.

5. Homework Assignment—If a monthly Book Share has not been conducted recently, each child should bring a book to share with the class. This should be a book they think others in the class might like to read. Students need to be prepared to talk about the book and answer questions from classmates. This is an excellent way to introduce new material to the class and frequently gives the teacher ideas for books to order. The teacher should also be prepared to share a book.

6. Based on each child's Book Share material, students should each write about connections they made when reading the books.

7. Every child knows a lot about at least one topic. Being able to demonstrate that knowledge and expertise is a wonderful self-esteem booster. What better way could there be to model background knowledge than to allow students to be experts? By using Figure #3-2, children write what they know about three topics. Each is then given the opportunity to share their expertise with the entire class or a small group. The teacher should also model this activity on the overhead projector with areas of his/her own knowledge.

Background Knowledge

Use the three types of text connections to show how you use what you already know to understand what you read.

Directions: Read this story and make three connections.

Spencer was a great bike rider. He wanted to grow up to be a professional stunt rider and travel the world doing his bike tricks. He practiced every day in every kind of weather. He learned to jump off ramps and spin his bike around in the air. Spencer became the best biker in his town.

One day he jumped from the ramp at the bike park and missed his landing. He fell hard on the ground and rolled over and over. Two of his teeth were knocked out, and his ankle was hurt. From that day on, Spencer decided he would become a doctor instead of a biker.

Text-to-self connection _____

_____

_____

Text-to-text connection _____

_____

_____

Text-to-world connection _____

_____

_____

I'm an Expert!

Everyone knows a lot about something. Think of things you know about. Are there animals, people, games, places, or things to do that you really like?

Directions: Write three topics you know a lot about. Then write everything you can about each topic. You will share this information with the class, so think of interesting facts and background knowledge you have about each topic.

Topic #1 _____

I know these things: _____

_____

_____

_____

Topic #2 _____

I know these things: _____

_____

_____

_____

Topic #3 _____

I know these things: _____

_____

_____

_____

Quiz—Background Knowledge

1. What is background knowledge?

_____

_____

_____

_____

_____

2. What are the three text connections?

a. _____

_____

b. _____

_____

c. _____

_____

3. What is text?

_____

_____

_____

_____

_____

Name: _____

Figure #3-4

Reading Connection Newsletter

Dear Parents/Guardians:

This week in reading we learned about activating background knowledge and making text connections. In order to read well and comprehend, all readers must connect what is being read to what they already know. These connections can be text-to-self (what I have experienced or someone I know has experienced), text-to-text (what I have read or seen on TV or a movie), or text-to-world (what I know about the world around me). Students have practiced using the strategies in class with books and articles. Parents/guardians can model this technique by frequently saying "This reminds me of..." while reading or watching TV. This is a good reminder to link previous knowledge to new knowledge.

Next week we will be learning about generating questions while reading. Students will practice working with text by writing questions to be answered as they read. They will find that these questions help set a purpose for reading and give focus to their work.

Below you will find this week's reading log to be filled out and returned on Friday morning. Please remember that not every day will have home reading indicated. Just turn in as much as has been accomplished.

Please write the date next to each day.

Friday _____	Saturday _____	Sunday _____	Monday _____
Minutes read	Minutes read	Minutes read	Minutes read
_____	_____	_____	_____
Tuesday _____	Wednesday _____	Thursday _____	
Minutes read	Minutes read	Minutes read	
_____	_____	_____	

Student's name _____

Parent/Guardian signature _____ Date _____

Week 4—Questioning

Questioning while reading is a strategy all good readers use. Many do this without realizing it is being done. Students question the text, asking questions such as, "What is meant by that?" and "Is that really a fact or just the author's opinion?" They also question themselves, asking questions such as, "What would I have done if I were the character?" and "How does that relate to my experiences?" This provides the opportunity for readers to stop and think, reflect, and comment on the text. This is a strategy to cure the "I-don't-remember-what-I-read" problem many readers have. By stopping and questioning, students are taking the time to think and review. This leads to better retention of material being read.

In the previously cited book, *I Read It, But I Don't Get It,* Cris Tovani describes "ponderable and clarifying questions." Clarifying questions are those which need to be answered immediately for comprehension to occur. Without the answers, the rest of the text will become increasingly incomprehensible. For example, a reader who does not know that the characters in a book are actually animals and not humans will have difficulty understanding the plot, action, and story development. By stopping as soon as comprehension has become difficult and asking, "What don't I understand? What is not making sense?", a reader can re-read or ask for help.

> *Clarifying questions are those which need to be answered immediately for comprehension to occur.*
>
> *Ponderable questions are those that readers can take time answering.*

Ponderable questions, on the other hand, are those that readers can take time answering. The meaning of the whole text will still be apparent without answering these right away. "Is this character tall or short?" might not affect the comprehension of the material immediately. This is information that might or might not be divulged later in reading. It is not critical to understanding the text.

Students must understand that questioning the text as they read is like building the foundation of a house. Unless clarifying questions are answered, the whole building (comprehension) will crumble. By knowing, however, that not all questions must be answered immediately and that it is good to have questions about material, students can relax and read for meaning.

There are three major sources for answers to the questions students ask the text and themselves as they read.

1. Answers can be found in the book, article, or other material. Reading a little further will sometimes provide the answers.

2. Answers can also be found in the student's background knowledge. A reader's own schema can provide many answers. Most students in elementary school have yet to understand that they can be the source of solutions to questions.

3. Finally, readers can find answers in other sources such as dictionaries, encyclopedias, other text, the Internet, their peers, adults, etc. These other sources are valuable means of gaining comprehension.

Lessons and Activities

1. Model questioning techniques by reading text that is unfamiliar to the students. As you read aloud, stop frequently and ask questions. Model asking the author questions by saying, "What were you thinking about when you developed this character?" Model asking the book questions by saying, "Are you telling me that...?" Finally, model asking yourself questions as you read by starting with "I wonder...." Make comments frequently about what you are reading, such as, "Wow! I didn't expect that to happen." Setting examples of how to ask questions about the text will make the students see it as a part of what good readers do and will make it easier for them to try this strategy in their own reading.

2. Direct students to read and complete Figure #4-1, which tells a story and questions as it proceeds. This gives practice in stopping to think about what is being read.

3. Discuss writing questions while reading. If students are reading material on which they cannot write or make marks, how can they record questions? Distribute small "sticky notes," and practice using them for question/comment recording. Ask each student to use the material they are currently reading, and practice writing questions and comments on the notes and stick them in the book so they extend beyond the page to be easily found later. Explain that as the questions are answered, the notes can be removed. They should save these notes for a later lesson. Figure #4-2 is an activity on which students can practice writing questions and comments as they read a text.

4. Using the sticky notes reflecting questions that were answered in the previous activity, ask students to break into pairs or small groups to discuss where they found the answers to their questions. Did they look up the answer in another source, figure it out for themselves, or discover it as they read further in the text? Which sources were used most? Were there questions that were never answered? Were they clarifying questions that obstructed meaning or ponderable questions that could be left unanswered?

5. Role-play author and reader. Working in pairs, students choose a favorite book or fairy tale. One child acts as the author and one as the reader of that particular text. Together they write questions and answers about the story and present it to the class as a short performance. Most students enjoy acting, and being able to work cooperatively with another child takes the anxiety out of this activity for anyone who is unsure about participating.

Questioning the Text

While you read, you should stop and ask questions. Write your questions in the margin of the book, on sticky notes, or on a piece of paper. You might also write words that you do not know. You might want to write comments telling how you feel about what you are reading.

Directions: Read the story below. Ask questions, make comments, and write unfamiliar vocabulary words in the boxes to the right. The first one is done for you.

Kelly was a small, black and white dog. He lived with the Smith family on a farm. Kelly's best friend was Tommy Smith, the youngest child in the family. The two played all day in the fields and the barnyard. One day Tommy could not find Kelly. He asked his mother, his father, and his brothers and sisters if they had seen the dog. No one knew where Kelly was.

> *What kind of dog is he?*

Tommy looked in all of Kelly's favorite hiding places. No Kelly. He searched the fields and in the barn. Still no Kelly. Finally, Tommy had to give up. Kelly must have run away.

At last, Tommy heard a small "meow." He followed the sound to the hall closet. There was a mother cat and five beautiful kittens all snuggled on an old sweater. Standing next to them was Kelly! He was guarding the new kittens.

Name: _____

Figure #4-2

Practice Questioning the Text

Directions: As you read the book your teacher assigns, think of questions and comments you have in your head. Write the questions, vocabulary words, and comments in the left column below. Think about what kinds of questions you have written. Where can you find the answers?

	Page # _____ I can find the answer in _____
	Page # _____ I can find the answer in _____
	Page # _____ I can find the answer in _____

Quiz—Questioning the Text

1. Why do you need to question text?

   _____

   _____

   _____

2. What are clarifying questions?

   _____

   _____

   _____

3. What are ponderable questions?

   _____

   _____

   _____

4. When you can't write in a book you are reading, where can you write your questions?

   _____

   _____

   _____

5. Name three places to find answers to your questions

   a. _____

   b. _____

   c. _____

Name: _____

Figure #4-4

Reading Connection Newsletter

Dear Parents/Guardians:

This week in reading we learned about questioning the text. Good readers must constantly be thinking about what they are reading. Questioning the book, making comments, and looking for unknown vocabulary are all strategies for developing thinking skills in reading. We also learned how to know if a question needs to be answered immediately in order to comprehend the material or if the answer can be found later while still understanding what is being read. There are three places to find answers to our questions: in the book; in our background knowledge; or in another source such as dictionaries, the Internet, or asking other people. Please watch to see if your child is writing notes as they read to practice this strategy.

Next week's focus will be main idea. The students will learn how to determine the most important point in whatever text they are reading. This is a skill that will make reading relevant and understandable.

As always, plenty of reading should be done at home. A minimum of 15 minutes per day should be a good goal at this point.

Below you will find this week's reading log to be filled out and returned on Friday morning. Thank you.

Please write the date next to each day.

Friday _____	Saturday _____	Sunday _____	Monday _____
Minutes read	Minutes read	Minutes read	Minutes read
_____	_____	_____	_____
Tuesday _____	Wednesday _____	Thursday _____	
Minutes read	Minutes read	Minutes read	
_____	_____	_____	

Student's name _____

Parent/Guardian signature _____ Date _____

Week 5—Main Idea

Word Attack!
2-letter consonant blends (tr, cl, etc.)

By this time in the school year, the class should be working on learning reading skills in the context of literature. Lessons and activities suggested will frequently refer to "the class novel or book," meaning the literature being used with the whole class or in ability-grouped clusters of students. The worksheets and activities can be used with all students, regardless of the level of the material.

Most teachers would agree that the concept of main idea is vital in reading comprehension. Some would go so far as to say it is the most important key to understanding reading. Certainly, knowing the most important point in the text is essential and includes understanding of many other concepts outlined in this book such as details, sequence, and determining importance.

The focus of lessons this week should be on what the main idea is and how to determine it. Teachers are encouraged to use poetry, newspapers, books, Internet material, fairy tales, plays, and any other text available to add to the enjoyment and understanding of the concept. This is knowledge that makes reading meaningful in all contexts.

Main idea is the central objective in writing, and reading, any text. The question most teachers ask when teaching this concept is, "What is this all about?" Students need to sift through all the details to get to the kernel of importance, which is the main idea. Students may get lost in the supporting and related details, assigning them great importance and missing the most important point. By basing instruction on simple text first and moving on to more complex material, teachers can scaffold this learning and make it more logical. "What is *The Three Little Pigs* about? Tell me in one sentence." By reducing text to one phrase or sentence, students find the main idea.

Lessons and Activities

1. Discuss the meaning of main idea. Practice finding it in nursery rhymes and fairy tales. Talk about a read-aloud book that has been read to the class. Discuss how to find the main idea. Students should look for the major "umbrella" under which all details are included. Draw an umbrella with "The Main Idea" written across the top. Underneath this, let students write details and ideas that support this concept.

2. Students complete Figure #5-1, reading a short article and answering questions about main idea.

3. Breaking down material into smaller passages is often helpful in determining main idea. Figure #5-2 can be used in reading groups or as a class activity incorporating the current class novel or read-aloud book. Students will have the opportunity to look for the most important point being made by the author, page-by-page. This activity is excellent when used on an overhead projector or board as the reading is being done. Group members can contribute their thoughts orally, rather than in writing.

4. Practice choosing the main idea for each short passage on Figure #5-3.

5. Main idea is not always explicitly stated. Students must try to determine the most important point by putting together clues in the text or in a picture. Ask students to look at pictures you have distributed (newspaper photos are excellent examples) and make up titles for the pictures that reflect the main idea.

Main Idea Practice

The main idea is what the text is all about. It is the author's most important message to the reader.

Directions: Read the story in the box. Then answer the questions about main idea.

I think dolphins are very interesting animals. On a visit to Florida, my family went to Sea World and saw lots of dolphins. We learned that they are mammals and must breathe air to live. They have live babies. Dolphins eat fish. Killer whales are related to dolphins. When we petted the dolphins, we found that they have very smooth skin and they like to be touched. Since our trip, dolphins have become my favorite animals.

1. The main idea of this story is _____

_____.

2. Two clues that showed the main idea are

a. _____

_____

b. _____

_____

Finding the Main Idea

Directions: Each page of a story can have a main idea, which together will tell the main idea of the whole story. Read what the teacher assigns, one page at a time. Fill out the chart below, telling the main idea of each page.

Title of book: _____

Page number	Main idea of this page

Find the Main Idea

Directions: Read the paragraphs and choose the main idea for each one.

1. Lunchtime was very noisy in the school cafeteria. Every day students yelled and were rude to each other. One day, Jason decided to sit quietly and only whisper. Soon the other kids at his table did the same thing. The next day, the children at the next table were quiet, too. In a few days, the whole cafeteria was a quieter, nicer place.

   The main idea of this paragraph is:
   a. Jason had lots of friends.
   b. Milk is healthy to drink at lunch.
   c. Lunch tastes good in the cafeteria.
   d. One person can make big changes.

2. Marisol found a yellow kitten on the way to school. It didn't have a collar and seemed to be lost. Marisol knew she could not bring the cat to school. All day in class she thought about the kitten and wondered if it would still be there when she walked home. She did not do a good job on her work in school because she was lost in thought about the kitten.

   The main idea of this paragraph is:
   a. A kitten makes a good pet.
   b. Yellow is a good color for a cat.
   c. Marisol was not a good student.
   d. Marisol could not work in school because she was thinking about the kitten.

3. When Mark went gold panning in the mountains, he used a flat pan to scoop up water in a mountain stream. Next, he learned to move the water in the pan around and around to make the heavy pieces of rock settle to the bottom. Mark found some small pieces of gold in the pan.

   The main idea of this paragraph is:
   a. Gold is very beautiful.
   b. Mark went gold panning.
   c. It is fun in the mountains.
   d. Mark went to the mountains.

Quiz—Main Idea

1. What is the main idea of a text?

   _____

   _____

   _____

2. What is the main idea of the book we are reading in class?

   _____

   _____

   _____

3. Think of a fairy tale. In one sentence, write the main idea of the story.

   _____

   _____

   _____

4. What question should you ask yourself if you don't know the main idea of what you are reading?

   _____

   _____

   _____

5. Why is it important to know the main idea of what you are reading?

   _____

   _____

   _____

Name: _____

Figure #5-5

Reading Connection Newsletter

Dear Parents/Guardians:

Knowing the main idea of what is being read is important for all readers. The author's main point is what readers look for and need to know. This week we have been learning how to determine the main idea in text. Students have learned to ask themselves, "What is this all about?" and to condense their answer into one sentence to reflect the author's main point. After reading or watching a TV show or movie, ask your child to tell you the main idea. See if you have the same idea or if your perception differs.

Next week we will be learning about details. These are facts that support the main idea and make reading interesting, educational, and fun.

How is your child's home reading coming along? Students who are reading at home are making progress in class, too. If your child is reluctant to read at home, you might try "shared reading." You read one page, your child reads the next, taking turns to enjoy reading together. The time you spend sharing reading may be included in the reading log.

This week's log is, as usual, at the bottom of this page. Please be sure to send it to school next Friday morning. Not every day has to be filled in for credit. Thank you for your continued work helping your child to be a successful reader.

Please write the date next to each day.

Friday _____ Minutes read _____	Saturday _____ Minutes read _____	Sunday _____ Minutes read _____	Monday _____ Minutes read _____
Tuesday _____ Minutes read _____	Wednesday _____ Minutes read _____	Thursday _____ Minutes read _____	

Student's name _____

Parent/Guardian signature _____ Date _____

Week 6—Details

Supporting details describe or explain the main idea. They make reading interesting and informational. Students often find themselves so engrossed in details that they either miss the main idea or think that the descriptors are the topic. Using webs or story maps to teach about supporting aspects can help students see and visually conceptualize this idea.

Teaching about details naturally follows last week's lessons about main idea. "Who, what, when, where, why, and how" describe the major topic. Teaching the "5 W's and an H" and practicing writing, as well as reading, for this concept is an important step in developing comprehension of text.

Lessons and Activities

1. To introduce the topic, tell the story of *Goldilocks and the Three Bears* without supporting details. This will sound something like, "Goldilocks went to the bears' house and did some things she shouldn't have done. Then the bears came home." Ask students if that was interesting to them. Solicit their additional details and write them on the board. Sequence their ideas and add to what you initially said. Now, is the story more interesting? Do you know more about what happened?

2. Introduce the 5 W's and an H. Distribute Figure #6-1. Ask students to write the main idea of a fairy tale. Go around the classroom and check that they are writing only one sentence and that it is actually the main idea. Next, ask students to fill in the 5 W's and an H below the main idea. Teachers might want to model this activity on the board. Finally, discuss which details were the most difficult to find. Use these papers to assess individual problems with the concept of supporting details.

3. Distribute Figure #6-2 on which students will read a paragraph and identify the 5 W's and an H.

4. Distribute six slips of paper to each student. Ask them to write a "who" on the first, a "what" on the second, and so forth until they have one for each of the 5 W's and an H. Collect the slips, putting each in a box labeled Who, What, When, etc. Stir the contents of each box and allow each child to pull out one slip from each of the six boxes. Then direct the students to write a story using all six elements. This is a very enjoyable activity which can result in very funny stories being written. The stories might not make much sense, but the idea of incorporating the details is utilized in a fun way.

5. Details are necessary to all content material students are learning in class. Ask them to write important details about their science, social studies, and math lessons. Are these supporting elements or main ideas? Begin to fill a bulletin board or chart with the details they have found in other subjects.

6. Discuss how newspaper articles are written. The main idea should be in the first, or topic, sentence. The first one or two paragraphs should contain the 5 W's. The rest of the article should outline the H, or How. Model looking for these supporting details in an article on the overhead projector. Underline or highlight the 5 W's with different colored pens. Discuss looking for the How in the rest of the article.

Distribute a photocopied newspaper article. Ask students to use markers or colored pencils to underline or highlight as you did on the example. Discuss class answers.

7. Detail cards are an entertaining activity. After reading a selection that contains many details, students fill out index cards with individual facts learned while reading. They may also draw a picture representing the fact on the card. Sort the facts, putting together all similar responses. Compare and contrast the cards.

Supporting Details

Directions: Write the title and one-sentence main idea of a fairy tale on the lines below. Then write the who, what, when, where, why, and how details of the story.

Title: _____

Main idea (one sentence): _____

_____.

Who? _____

_____

What? (What did they do or what happened?) _____

_____

When? _____

_____

Where? _____

_____

Why? _____

_____

How? _____

_____

Finding Details

Directions: Read the story below. Find the who, what, when, where, why, and how of the story. Write the details on the lines.

A Wish Come True

Tony lived in Denver. He wanted an X-Box more than anything in the world. He asked his parents to buy him one every day. His father finally told him that he must earn the money to buy one for himself. Tony did jobs for everyone he knew. He shoveled snow, walked dogs, and babysat little children. Finally, he had the money he needed. He bought his X-Box and knew that it was important because he had earned it for himself.

Who? _____

What? _____

_____

When? (Look for a clue in the story.) _____

Where? _____

Why? _____

_____

How? _____

_____

Quiz—Details

1. What are supporting details?

   _____

   _____

   _____

2. What are the 5 W's and an H?

   a. _____

   b. _____

   c. _____

   d. _____

   e. _____

   f. _____

3. Why is it important to understand supporting details?

   _____

   _____

   _____

4. **Review question:** What is main idea?

   _____

   _____

   _____

Name: _____

Figure #6-4

Reading Connection Newsletter

Dear Parents/Guardians:

This week's reading topic was details. Supporting details describe and give information about the main idea. We learned about the 5 W's and an H (who, what, when, where, why, and how). Looking for details is very important in reading. Details give us information and enjoyment while learning about the main topic. Be sure to ask your child to tell you details about the main idea as he/she reads daily at home.

Please fill out the bottom of this page as your child reads at home this week. As always, return this sheet with the child's name and your signature on Friday morning for credit and rewards.

Thank you again for your support of literacy at home. Being a reading role model is one of the most important things you can do to ensure your child's success in school.

Please write the date next to each day.

Friday _____	Saturday _____	Sunday _____	Monday _____
Minutes read	Minutes read	Minutes read	Minutes read
_____	_____	_____	_____
Tuesday _____	Wednesday _____	Thursday _____	
Minutes read	Minutes read	Minutes read	
_____	_____	_____	

Student's name _____

Parent/Guardian signature _____ Date _____

Week 7—Visualization and Imagery

Visualizing text is a skill that does not come naturally to all children. Students whose learning style is very visual might get pictures in their minds of what they are reading, but others may not. Visualization is making a picture, or movie, in the mind while reading. Imagery is language that appeals to the five senses. This topic is interesting for children, as it opens up a new way to comprehend text.

Good readers visualize constantly as they read. They "see" the characters and settings. They watch a moving picture play as the action of the book or written directions unfolds. Once students learn these skills, reading becomes much more enjoyable and text is easier to remember. Instead of having only words to rely on for recalling material, students can call on pictures they have designed in their minds. Drawings and oral descriptions can make visualization easy to learn. The following lessons and activities are helpful in accomplishing this.

Lessons and Activities

1. Find a particularly vivid description of a person, place, or thing in a book. Ask students to close their eyes while you read. When finished, ask "What did you see?" Describe visualization as making a mental picture or movie in your head. Read the selected material again. This time ask students to draw a picture as you read, keeping in mind the details the author has written. Discuss the pictures they have drawn.

2. Distribute Figure #7-1. Students will read the short passage and draw a picture at the bottom of the page illustrating the creature described in the paragraph. It is fun to compare students' pictures.

3. Divide the class into small groups. Give each group a piece of butcher paper large enough that the students can sit side-by-side with blank paper in front of each one. Explain that you are going to read a story which they will be illustrating. Begin with the child sitting at the far left side of the paper. Read the first part of the story and have that child draw what he/she visualizes. Then read the next part and have the child immediately to the first child's right draw what he/she imagined. Continue until the story is finished and each child has drawn. Ask students to each retell their portion of the story to their small group.

4. Imagery is language that appeals to the five senses. To teach this lesson successfully, the students' background knowledge must include the five senses. Be sure this knowledge is in place before beginning the next activity. Model writing a paragraph that makes the reader use all five senses. A great tool for doing this is writing about making popcorn. Discuss what setting or situations would be most likely to utilize all five senses. List these on the board. The list might include a kitchen, circus, restaurant, etc. Then ask students to write a paragraph using their senses to describe a place or experience. Share these in class.

5. Using a book read in class, have each student complete Figure #7-2. Students choose a descriptive passage or chapter and illustrate it using the clues the author has written.

6. Students' visualizations can be used all year to decorate the classroom. This is a good representation of individual books and the images students had as they read.

7. Visualization can be used in reading for all subjects. As a group, practice visualizing text from other subjects. Remind students to get a picture in their minds as they are reading various content material.

What Do You See?

Directions: Read the story about a creature. Draw the creature at the bottom of the page. You may look back to the paragraph for help.

Jimmy's Bad Dream

Jimmy had a dream about a terrible creature that came to school. It was green with pink dots. It had six legs and two heads. The monster's eyes were orange, and its ears were blue. Each foot had four yellow claws. The monster had a very mean look on its face. When Jimmy woke up, he was glad it had been just a dream.

Draw the monster from Jimmy's dream. Make it look exactly how it was described.

Draw What You Read

Directions: Choose a description you have read in a book in class. Write the author's words. Draw what you saw in your mind as you read.

Title of book: _____

Author's description: _____

_____

_____

_____

_____

Your visualization:

_____
| |
| |
| |
| |
| |
| |
| |
| |

Quiz—Visualization and Imagery

1. What is visualization?

   _____

   _____

   _____

   _____

2. Why do good readers use visualization?

   _____

   _____

   _____

   _____

3. What is imagery?

   _____

   _____

   _____

   _____

4. What are the five senses?

   a. _____

   b. _____

   c. _____

   d. _____

   e. _____

Name: _____

Figure #7-4

Reading Connection Newsletter

Dear Parents/Guardians:

We have learned about visualization and imagery this week. It is important for good readers to get pictures or movies in their heads as they read. This leads to better comprehension and easier retention of the material. We practiced making pictures on paper and in our minds to illustrate authors' words. We also learned that this is a strategy that is essential to use in other areas, such as science and social studies. Math problems can be visualized, too, making them easier to understand.

Imagery is language that uses the five senses to make text easier to comprehend. We learned about the five senses and how to recognize their use in writing and reading.

Thank you for helping your child with the weekly reading log at the bottom of this page.

Please write the date next to each day.

Friday _____	Saturday _____	Sunday _____	Monday _____
Minutes read	Minutes read	Minutes read	Minutes read
_____	_____	_____	_____
Tuesday _____	Wednesday _____	Thursday _____	
Minutes read	Minutes read	Minutes read	
_____	_____	_____	

Student's name _____

Parent/Guardian signature _____ Date _____

Week 8—Cause and Effect

Modeling is an effective way to introduce cause and effect. Hold a full glass of water over a pail. Ask the students what will happen if you tip the glass over. They will answer that the water will spill into the pail. Next, stand up dominos in a line and ask what the students think will happen if you push over the first domino. Do this with several examples. Then ask, "What caused the water to spill, the dominos to fall, etc.?" Explain that the cause is what makes something happen. We can say the water spilled because we tipped the glass. What happens as a result of our actions is called the effect. Elicit several more examples by asking students to pose questions that begin with the word "why." List the effects and their causes on the board.

Move on to relating cause and effect to reading. Using a story such as *Cinderella*, ask the children to finish this sentence: "Cinderella could not go to the ball because...." Write the cause (her stepsisters and stepmother would not let her go) and the effect (Cinderella could not go to the ball) on the board under the headings of Cause and Effect. Continue this exercise with more examples from books the students have read. Explain that understanding cause and effect makes comprehending the material easier. Ask students to give examples from their own reading. The basic concept is that one thing happens that makes another happen. The first is the cause, the second is the effect.

Knowing how to recognize cause and effect will strengthen comprehension by helping students link events in their reading to each other and to background knowledge. As with most of the reading skills and strategies in this book, prior knowledge (schema) is essential to making sense of what is being read.

Lessons and Activities

1. One very enjoyable activity to develop a sense of cause and effect is to make a "string of effects." This teaches not only the basic concept of cause and effect, but that every effect can become a cause. Begin by writing something that could happen at the top of the board, for example, "I did not do my homework." Draw a short line down from this statement and ask students to tell what the effect of this might be. Write their response, which might be, "I did not do well on a test." Draw a short line down from this statement and again ask students to tell what the effect might be, such as "My parents grounded me." Continue this to the bottom of the board. Keep pointing out that each effect becomes a cause of the next action. Ask students to write their own "string of effects" in Figure #8-1.

2. An effect can have many causes. For example, the birthday party was fun because the food was good, the games were fun, the gifts were great, etc. Likewise, a cause can have many effects. For example, because the children were noisy, no one could hear the teacher, recess was cancelled, etc. Draw a web on the board with an effect in the middle and lines out to the many causes. Ask students to fill in the blanks. Next draw a web with a cause in the middle and ask students to fill in the possible effects.

3. Ask students to complete Figure #8-2 indicating either the cause or effect, as directed. Go over these as a class. Answers will vary according to students' background knowledge and experiences.

4. Write a cause on a large index card, marked "Cause." On a matching card, write the effect and label this card "Effect." Do this with several examples, ensuring that each student will have a card. Ask someone with a cause card to read it to the class. The student with the matching effect should read his/her card and explain why it is a logical effect. Do this until the entire class has finished. Are there cards that could be used in more than one situation? Were there cards left over that do not match? How can this be fixed?

5. Cut pictures out of magazines or newspapers that illustrate effects, such as a car that has a dented fender. Ask students to write possible causes for these pictures. Remember that there may be several right answers. A child who has seen a deer hit by a car may say that is the cause of the dent. Another who has seen an accident in the city might say the cause was someone running a red light. Answers depend on individual schema.

6. Using your classroom library or the Media Center in your school, look for good examples of cause and effect in literature. Excellent illustrations of this concept in children's literature might include *Alexander and the Terrible, Horrible, No Good, Very Bad Day* by Judith Viorst and *If You Give a Mouse a Cookie* by Laura Numeroff. Read these books with the class and discuss the causes and effects found in them.

String of Effects

Cause and effect is when one thing happens that makes another thing happen.

Directions: Beginning with one thing that could happen in your life, write an effect of that happening. Then use that effect as a cause and tell what could happen next. Keep going until you reach the bottom of the page.

Cause _____

Effect #1 _____ then,

Effect #2 _____ then,

Effect #3 _____ then,

Effect #4 _____ then,

Effect #5 _____ then,

Effect #6 _____ .

If you can think of more in this string of effects, write them on the back of this page.

Name: _____   Figure #8-2

Cause and Effect

Directions: For each cause written below, write an effect. For each effect, write a cause.

Cause	**Effect**
1. The dog got out of the yard.	_____
2. School is out in June.	_____
3. _____	He got wet.
4. _____	The teacher was happy.
5. Mark did not do his homework.	_____
6. _____	We turned on the fan.
7. The snow was deep.	_____
8. _____	The girl cried.
9. _____	He covered his ears.
10. The match was hot.	_____

Quiz—Cause and Effect

1. What is cause and effect?

   _____

   _____

   _____

   _____

   _____

2. Write a string of effects with at least one cause to start and five effects in order.

   Cause _____

   Effect _____ then,

   Effect _____ then,

   Effect _____ then,

   Effect _____ then,

   Effect _____.

3. Write about a cause and effect from one book we have read in class.

   _____

   _____

   _____

   _____

Name: _____

Figure #8-4

Reading Connection Newsletter

Dear Parents/Guardians:

    As we continue our studies of reading comprehension skills, this week we learned about cause and effect. This concept is basic to all reading and, of course, to life. When one thing happens, it makes another thing happen. We have made "strings of effects," which show how one effect becomes a cause to another effect and so on. Using this in the context of good books, we have learned to look for cause and effect and how to increase our comprehension of reading material through the use of this strategy. In daily reading at home we need to be thinking about this and pointing out the causes and effects of characters' actions.

    Next week we will be learning about sequence. There are many kinds of sequence, and we will discover how sequence can make us better readers.

    Please fill out the reading log below daily and return it to school on Friday morning. If you find a log at home that was not returned, please send it in now for credit.

Please write the date next to each day.

Friday _____	Saturday _____	Sunday _____	Monday _____
Minutes read	Minutes read	Minutes read	Minutes read
_____	_____	_____	_____
Tuesday _____	Wednesday _____	Thursday _____	
Minutes read	Minutes read	Minutes read	
_____	_____	_____	

Student's name _____

Parent/Guardian signature _____ Date _____

Week 9—Sequence

By this time in elementary school, most students have learned about sequence. However, they have not always discovered the importance of sequence in their reading. A review of this important concept is necessary in every grade because of the significance it has in every subject covered in every grade. Sequence ties together all the happenings in a book and all directions given in a logical order, which helps students organize the text and their own thoughts.

Introducing sequence simply as "order" is straightforward. Pointing out examples of sequence can and should be done consistently throughout the school year. Keep in mind that sequence is not just found in reading class. It is a part of everything being taught and learned all year.

Lessons and Activities

1. Types of sequence are size, numerical, alphabetical, chronological, and importance. After describing these, ask students to give examples. Line up students according to various sequences.

2. Have students make time lines of their lives. These can be embellished with photographs, drawn on large paper, decorated, or simply written on notebook paper. Allow sufficient time to share this finished assignment in class. These are reflections of students' lives and are very important to them. It is also good to display these in the classroom where students can enjoy their work.

3. Distribute comic strips that have been cut into individual panels and mixed up. Let children assemble them like puzzles to make sense. Talk about what a difference sequence makes in such instances. Allow students to switch puzzles with each other until everyone has had the opportunity to see several.

4. Alphabetical order is an essential skill to learn and master. By writing the alphabet in a column on the board and asking students to name a food, game, or book that begins with each letter, the use of alphabetical order is entrenched in a pleasant way.

5. Assign Figure #9-1, asking students to read the sentences, then write 1 next to the first event, 2 next to the second, etc. Then students can write the complete story in the correct order at the bottom of the page.

6. Divide the class into small groups of three or four students. Give each group an envelope containing several index cards. On each card should be a sentence that is part of a logical paragraph. Students decide in their groups what order the sentences should be placed to make sense. Rotate the envelopes through all the groups.

7. Using a picture from a magazine or newspaper, ask the students to write a story in logical sequence about what happened after the picture was taken. Note: This ties in with last week's study of cause and effect. Distribute pictures for each child to write a story.

8. Ask students to put the classroom library in order by alphabetical sequence. This should be by title, not author. Make sure the children understand not to use "the," "a," or "an" as the first word in the titles. Warning: This is a noisy activity that incorporates a lot of cooperative work. Plan with the students in advance how this will work.

Sequence

Directions: Read the sentences below. Then find the one that should be first and write the numeral 1 next to it. Find the next sentence and write 2. Keep going through 5. Then write the story in the correct order at the bottom of the page to make sure the sequence makes sense.

_____   Finally, she found the very pair she had been looking for.

_____   Beth needed new shoes for the big basketball game.

_____   She tried on many pairs that were just not right.

_____   Beth wore her shoes to the next game.

_____   She went to the store with her mother.

Now, write the story in order here:

_____

_____

_____

_____

_____

_____

_____

_____

_____

_____

_____

Quiz—Sequence

1. What is sequence?

_____

_____

2. How do good readers use sequence?

_____

_____

3. Tell how you use each type of sequence:

a. time sequence

_____

_____

b. size sequence

_____

_____

c. alphabetical order

_____

_____

d. numerical order

_____

_____

e. importance sequence

_____

_____

Reading Connection Newsletter

Dear Parents/Guardians:

We have had a lot of fun this week learning about sequence. The time lines of students' lives that were worked on at home were excellent examples of sequence and are now on display in the classroom. Thank you for helping with dates, etc. We learned how important sequence is in our reading. This is a skill we will use in all aspects of our lives.

Next week we will learn the important strategy of comparing and contrasting.

Please fill out the reading log at the bottom of this page and return it to school next Friday morning. Thank you.

- -

Please write the date next to each day.

Friday _____ Minutes read _____	Saturday _____ Minutes read _____	Sunday _____ Minutes read _____	Monday _____ Minutes read _____
Tuesday _____ Minutes read _____	Wednesday _____ Minutes read _____	Thursday _____ Minutes read _____	

Student's name _____

Parent/Guardian signature _____ Date _____

Week 10—Compare and Contrast

Comparing and contrasting is a very important skill. It reflects knowledge at many levels. In order to compare, one must know details, identify similarities and differences, identify important characteristics, and organize information. These are relatively sophisticated tasks for students in grades 3–5, but can be taught through the use of graphic organizers such as Venn diagrams and compare/contrast matrices.

The results of teaching compare and contrast are improved mental organization and attention to detail while reading. These, in turn, lead to better retention of information and deeper understanding of text.

Lessons and Activities

1. Discuss what comparing and contrasting mean. "Compare" is used more commonly to mean finding similarities and differences. The term "contrast" means to find what is different between two or more things. Have students line up in the middle of the room. Explain that you are going to make a statement. The students who agree will move to one side of the room, those who disagree to the other. Undecided votes will stay in the middle. Think of topics about which students generally have strong opinions such as school uniforms, bedtimes, and food. Make a statement and ask students to move to the appropriate spots to indicate their agreement or disagreement. Compare and contrast the two groups. Write the results on the board. Make another statement and repeat the activity. When finished, compare and contrast the results. Brainstorm other topics to use with this activity. Save this list for tomorrow.

2. Demonstrate making a matrix (graph) with the things to be compared/contrasted across the top and important characteristics written down the side. Explain that this will help students visualize what is being compared. Give students Figure #10-1 to make their own matrix. Suggested topics could be types of dogs with characteristics such as size, friendliness, cost, etc., as the basis of comparison.

3. Using the newspaper, find examples of compare/contrast matrices. *USA Today* generally is a great resource for these materials, comparing a wide variety of things in colorful charts and graphs.

4. Present a number of different compare/contrast charts including bar graphs, line graphs, and pie charts. Ask the students to "read" the charts and explain how the strategy of compare and contrast was used.

5. Introduce Venn diagrams. These overlapping circles contain the exclusive characteristics of one thing being compared in the left portion of the chart and of the other in the right portion. The overlapping part in the middle reflects the similarities of the two. Model making such a diagram comparing cats and dogs. Discuss what students believe to be the same and different between these two animals.

Divide the class into pairs of students. Give them a Venn diagram to complete comparing themselves with their partners. Label the diagram with a name on each side and "Both" in the middle. Allow extra time for this activity, as students will want to talk about their shared interests and individual characteristics. Share as a class when finished.

6. Discuss how comparing and contrasting is important in building good reading skills. Compare characters, settings, etc., of books being used in class. Ask each student to complete Figure #10-2, comparing two books they have read.

Compare and Contrast Matrix

A matrix is a graph that shows how two or more things are alike or different.

Directions: Complete this matrix comparing two things you know something about.

	One thing to be compared: _____	Other thing to be compared: _____
One characteristic: _____		
Another characteristic: _____		
Another characteristic: _____		
Another characteristic: _____		

Compare and Contrast Books

Directions: Choose two books you have read. Use this compare and contrast matrix to write what is the same and different about them.

	Book 1 Title: _____ _____	Book 2 Title: _____ _____
Main Character(s)		
Setting		
Hard or easy to read		
Type of book: fiction or nonfiction		

Quiz—Compare and Contrast

1. What does it mean to compare and contrast?

_____

_____

_____

_____

2. Draw a comparison matrix and show what goes across the top and what goes down the side.

3. Draw a Venn diagram and label the parts.

4. Why is it important to compare and contrast while reading?

_____

_____

_____

_____

Name: _____

Figure #10-4

Reading Connection Newsletter

Dear Parents/Guardians:

We have had a busy week learning how to compare and contrast. We learned that finding differences and similarities is an important skill to use when we read. We made Venn diagrams and compare and contrast matrices. Be sure to ask to see this work.

Next week we will work on classification and categorization. This will be an interesting strategy to learn, and we will have a lot of enjoyable activities to take part in during the lessons.

Please fill out the weekly at-home reading log at the bottom of this page and return it on Friday morning. Thank you.

Please write the date next to each day.

Friday _____	Saturday _____	Sunday _____	Monday _____
Minutes read	Minutes read	Minutes read	Minutes read
_____	_____	_____	_____
Tuesday _____	Wednesday _____	Thursday _____	
Minutes read	Minutes read	Minutes read	
_____	_____	_____	

Student's name _____

Parent/Guardian signature _____ Date _____

Week 11—Classification and Categorization

Classification is another skill that students need, not only in reading, but in all facets of their lives. Being able to sort, categorize, and organize materials, items, and ideas is basic to all learning. Remembering information is made easier by organizing that knowledge in an easily-retrieved way.

In reading literature, students classify facts and ideas. Good characters, bad characters, motives, and actions are all concepts that are filed away in readers' minds to assist in comprehension. Teaching classification is important to developing this skill.

Lessons and Activities

1. The best way to start teaching classification is to actually categorize the students themselves. Be sure to do this in a way that will not make any child feel different than others or cause hurt feelings. Without explaining what you are doing, move girls to one side of the room and boys to the other. Ask what is being done. Explain that boys and girls are categories. Next, people with light-colored hair and dark hair can be sorted. Ask for examples of common denominators by which students can be categorized. What else in the room can be sorted this way? Practice sorting these objects.

2. Prepare index cards, each with a concept or thing written on the front. Examples might be dogs, places, people, foods, or games. Give each student a different card. Ask them to list at least ten things that could be in that specific category. Then let each student bring his or her list to the front of the class and read the list they have prepared. Other students may guess the category. This can also be played as partners in a manner similar to "Pyramid" on television. This game is very popular, and students will want to play it long after this unit is finished.

3. Assign Figure #11-1 on which the students will read a group of words and sort them into categories. This is a good sheet to use as homework, as it will very graphically show parents/guardians what is being learned in class.

4. Take a walk around the school. What categories of things do the students observe? Come back to class and write the categories and things that fit into those classifications on the board. These might include people, colors, sounds, etc.

5. Taking Figure #11-1 one step further, assign Figure #11-2. This time the students look at the items in each list and decide what the category name would be. Share these as a group when individual work is finished.

6. A word picture activity, such as Figure #11-3, is entertaining work for students. After they have colored the boxes by categories, they will have a pattern, word, or picture. Figure #11-3 will result in a pattern. Teachers may want to be creative and make this work produce a picture.

7. A quiz is provided for this section; however, another way of assessing this concept is to have objects on a table for individual students to classify. This is a chance for students to explain their thinking. Some may sort things in a highly creative or unusual way that could not be demonstrated on a paper and pencil test.

Sorting

Directions: Write the words below in the list where they belong.

apple	chair	cat	teacher	Scrabble®
dominoes	bird	pilot	table	bread
painter	cheese	dog	football	bed
turtle	policeman	hockey	lamp	hamburger

Category 1—Pets

_____

_____

_____

_____

Category 2—Foods

_____

_____

_____

_____

Category 3—Jobs

_____

_____

_____

_____

Category 4—Games

_____

_____

_____

_____

Category 5—Furniture

_____

_____

_____

_____

What's My Category?

Directions: Read each list of words below. Write the name of the category the list fits. Think about what the words have in common.

Items	Category
1. boats, trains, cars, airplanes	_____
2. United States, Mexico, Canada, France	_____
3. apples, bananas, grapes, oranges	_____
4. pencils, crayons, markers, pens	_____
5. trees, bushes, flowers, grass	_____
6. peas, carrots, potatoes, beans	_____
7. Mary, Sue, Jennifer, Lisa	_____
8. cloudy, snowy, rainy, cold	_____
9. reading, math, science, art	_____
10. north, south, east, west	_____
11. cows, horses, chickens, pigs	_____
12. parrots, canaries, robins, parakeets	_____
13. shoes, pants, sweaters, coats	_____
14. English, Spanish, Russian, French	_____
15. balls, nets, bats, pucks	_____

Find the Pattern

Directions: Sort the words by coloring each box.

Color **red** all the things that you might find in school.
Color **blue** all the things that have legs.
Color **green** all the things that you can eat.
Color **yellow** all the things that are transportation.

CAR	TRAIN	SPIDER	LION
BIKE	JET	CHAIR	ANT
SCOOTER	BOAT	PEOPLE	BIRD
SKATES	CANOE	POODLE	LIZARD
PENCILS	BOOKS	FRUIT	BEEF
PAPER	MARKERS	CANDY	CORN
TEACHER	STUDENTS	BEANS	ROLLS
SCISSORS	CLOCK	GRAPES	TACO

Quiz—Classification and Categorization

1. What is a category?

_____

_____

_____

_____

2. Why is it important to use classification?

_____

_____

_____

3. Write the names of three categories. Write five things that belong in each category.

Category 1: _____ **Category 2:** _____ **Category 3:** _____

1. _____   1. _____   1. _____

2. _____   2. _____   2. _____

3. _____   3. _____   3. _____

4. _____   4. _____   4. _____

5. _____   5. _____   5. _____

Name: _____

Figure #11-5

Reading Connection Newsletter

Dear Parents/Guardians:

Classifying information is a skill we all use every day. This week we learned to classify things and ideas. Knowing how to do this helps us in comprehending what we read. We are able to put ideas into groups that are easy to remember when we need to recall what was read. Categories also help us recognize how things we read go together. By putting similar thoughts and items together in our minds as we read, we can understand the relationships between major concepts in our texts.

Next week we will be learning to summarize and paraphrase what we read. This is an essential skill which we will practice all year and use in our at-home reading.

Please fill out the weekly reading log at the bottom of this page and return it on Friday morning. Thank you for supporting your child's reading at home.

Please write the date next to each day.

Friday _____ Minutes read _____	Saturday _____ Minutes read _____	Sunday _____ Minutes read _____	Monday _____ Minutes read _____
Tuesday _____ Minutes read _____	Wednesday _____ Minutes read _____	Thursday _____ Minutes read _____	

Student's name _____

Parent/Guardian signature _____ Date _____

Week 12—Summarizing and Paraphrasing

Summarizing is not only an important skill for students; it can be valuable to teachers in assessing children's comprehension of text. Retelling content reflects a student's ability to understand main idea, sequence, characters, plot, information, and instructions. By putting the text into their own words (paraphrasing), students develop their own interpretation of the material. By stopping while reading to summarize, children take the time to make sure comprehension is in place. By summarizing at the end of text, the entire meaning of the material can be put in place and organized for better retention of learning and checking for understanding. Summarizing also aids in eliminating the "I got to the end of the page, and I don't remember what I read" complaint when used after each paragraph. Students force themselves to remember as they go along rather than waiting until the end. Teachers should model summarizing and paraphrasing in their oral reading to children by stopping frequently to recap what has been read. Students should be instructed to do the same during and after reading. This strategy needs to be used by students in and out of school, for all classes, and for pleasure reading.

> *Retelling content reflects a student's ability to understand main idea, sequence, characters, plot, information, and instructions.*

Students' summary writing is an easy way for teachers to check for comprehension. Is the main idea present? What details did the students find important enough to include in the summary? Do fiction summaries include the characters, plot, setting, problem, solution, and point of view? Do nonfiction summaries include the topic, information, supporting details, and key vocabulary? Going over these summaries will give teachers an overall view of understanding.

Lessons and Activities

1. Explain that summarizing is a way to remember what has been read and put it into easier-to-remember language. Ask the students to choose a favorite song and write the lyrics in their own words. Try this with a folk or fairy tale. What kinds of things are important to be in the summary?

2. Complete Figure #12-1, paraphrasing nursery rhymes. Ask students to read their summaries out loud and see if their classmates can guess which nursery rhyme they are paraphrasing. If preferred, use a class novel or other book that all students have either read or listened to for this activity.

3. Give the students easy-to-read newspaper or magazine articles. *Time for Kids* and *Weekly Reader* are excellent resources for this type of material. Ask the children to summarize the articles. Discuss main idea and important details before beginning to write. In small groups, let students discuss their articles and compare summaries. Did one person feel that a detail was more important than another? Did someone think the main idea was different than others in the group? Encourage a free exchange of ideas with respect being shown to all members of the groups.

4. As students read, the teacher can call them to a quiet discussion place and ask for verbal summaries of the books they are reading. Figure #12-2 is a checklist to be kept for each student, detailing the oral retells and summaries given throughout the year. By keeping this chart for each child, the teacher can look at growth and needs in comprehension. This individual conference time can also be used to check oral reading skills and other concerns the teacher may have.

5. Students need to practice writing summaries to solidify this strategy in their minds. Using the class novel, have students choose several paragraphs to summarize, one at a time.

6. Cut interesting pictures out of magazines and newspapers. Ask students to write one-sentence summaries of what they see in the picture. This is good practice in keeping summaries short and free of many details.

7. Practice paraphrasing by reading a paragraph aloud to the students and asking them to put it into their own words. Expect a spirited discussion about what is important and what is not in the text.

Paraphrasing

Paraphrasing is summarizing something in your own words. It tells what the author means without using all the author's words.

Directions: Write these nursery rhymes in your own words.

1. Jack and Jill went up the hill
   To fetch a pail of water.
   Jack fell down and broke his crown,
   And Jill came tumbling after.

My words: _____

_____

_____

_____

2. Mary had a little lamb,
   Its fleece was white as snow.
   And everywhere that Mary went
   The lamb was sure to go.

My words: _____

_____

_____

_____

3. Jack Sprat could eat no fat.
   His wife could eat no lean.
   And so between the two of them
   They licked the platter clean.

My words: _____

_____

_____

_____

Figure #12-2

Summary Checklist

Student _____

Summary #____ Date _____

Title of text _____

Did the student include:

     _____ Main idea?

     _____ Characters?

     _____ Plot?

     _____ Important details?

     _____ Opinions about the text?

     _____ Other?

Teacher's comments _____

_____

_____

Summary # ____ Date _____

Title of text _____

Did the student include:

     _____ Main idea?

     _____ Characters?

     _____ Plot?

     _____ Important details?

     _____ Opinions about the text?

     _____ Other?

Teacher's comments _____

_____

_____

Quiz—Summarizing and Paraphrasing

1. What is a summary?

_____

_____

_____

_____

2. What is paraphrasing?

_____

_____

_____

_____

3. Why is it important to know how to summarize?

_____

_____

_____

_____

4. Write a one-sentence summary of the book you are reading in class.

_____

_____

_____

Name: _____

Figure #12-4

Reading Connection Newsletter

Dear Parents/Guardians:

Do you stop during or after reading to summarize what you have read? That is what we learned to do this week in class. Summarizing and paraphrasing (putting text into your own words) are important strategies. By stopping and thinking about what we read and putting it into one sentence, we will remember the main idea and important details. This is a skill that should be practiced during at-home reading. We need to stop about halfway down the page, summarize, and then do it again at the end of the page. Thanks for your help with this at home.

Please remember to fill out the bottom of this page and return the log to school on Friday morning. This extra practice at home can make such a big difference in reading skills.

- -

Please write the date next to each day.

Friday _____	Saturday _____	Sunday _____	Monday _____
Minutes read	Minutes read	Minutes read	Minutes read
_____	_____	_____	_____
Tuesday _____	Wednesday _____	Thursday _____	
Minutes read	Minutes read	Minutes read	
_____	_____	_____	

Student's name _____

Parent/Guardian signature _____ Date _____

Week 13—Context Clues

Using context clues to find the meaning of unknown words in reading is not a guessing game. It is a strategy that all readers, adults and children, use to make sense of text. Children use context clues first in listening to people speak. They do not know the definition of each word, but they use the words and phrases around the unknown words to figure out the meaning. Likewise, in reading, students must use the words, phrases, and sentences around new vocabulary to determine the definition. Learning how to use context clues alleviates the frustration of being stuck on a word and provides hints or clues about meanings.

There are two major types of context clues: direct and indirect. The direct clues are easily taught when students are instructed to look for "the-meaning-is-right-here" words. Words and phrases like *is*, *are*, *are called*, *means*, *or*, and *such as*, or words put into parentheses, are telling the readers that the definition is "right here." An example might be "The bongos, or small drums, were Jose's favorite to play." Students might not know what bongos are, but they can visualize small drums and get meaning from reading the sentence.

Indirect context clues are a bit more difficult, as they require the use of background knowledge and careful reading. The indirect clues to definitions of unknown words are found in the words, phrases, and sentences around those words. These clues do not give the exact meaning or a synonym; they hint at the definition. An example of an indirect context clue is, "Although John liked large dogs, he found the sheltie a good choice for his pet." Readers realize that the sheltie is unlike what John usually likes, so it must be a small dog. Approaching this as detective work is an enjoyable way for students to practice.

Before working with direct and indirect context clues, students should ask themselves if the word is really important to what they are reading. Should they take the time to figure out the word? Some criteria for deciding might be:

- Does not knowing this word keep me from understanding the main idea?

- Is the word repeated throughout the text?

- Am I frustrated by not knowing the word?

- Is the word obviously important (in the title, bold words, etc.)?

- When I say "blank" instead of the word, can I still comprehend the text?

Asking these questions can make the importance of the definition obvious. If the word does not block comprehension, it might be all right to go on reading without defining it. If it occurs again in the text, it might be time to figure out the word.

A word of advice: Students should know that they do not have to be able to pronounce the unknown word if they can surmise the definition and continue reading with comprehension.

Lessons and Activities

1. After a class discussion of context clues, provide practice in determining what words make sense in sentences. On Figure #13-1, ask students to fill in words that would be appropriate in the spaces. When finished, discuss this activity as a class, comparing and contrasting answers. Let students explain why they chose the words they did. Did the words make sense? Did students discover that there could be several different words that would be correct?

2. Instruct the use of initial and ending sounds in words as clues to what they might be. When added to the cloze activity above, the students have even more clues as to what the word might be. Figure #13-2 combines cloze and sounds to make choices even narrower. This activity might be more difficult for some students and could be a good choice as a cooperative lesson or small group instructional tool.

3. Putting together clues to find the meaning of words is the most difficult strategy in using context clues. Ask students to "play detective" to find the meanings of the bold-print words in Figure #13-3. By providing a multiple choice list, teachers are also giving students the chance to try words in the text and see if they make sense.

Fill in the Blanks

Directions: In each blank, write a word that makes sense. Think about the sentence and the words around the missing word. Does your word need an *s* on the end or an ending like *-ing* or *-ed?* Choose carefully.

One hot summer day my _____ and I decided to go _____ in the river. Our _____ had told us never to do _____. We were very, very _____ and figured we would be just _____.

When we got to the _____, we found a lot of _____. Everyone was having lots of _____. One group of _____ was swinging from a _____. They would swing out over the _____ and back to the _____. My _____ thought that _____ be fun, so he _____. When he swung back, he _____ his head and it began to _____.

By the time we got _____, he was better, but our _____ was very upset. She _____ us for a week, and we never _____ again.

Letters and Words

Directions: Fill in the blanks with words that make sense and have the beginning and ending sounds provided for you. Make sure your words seem right for what the sentence is saying.

Playing sports is a f_____te activity for many b_____s and girls. Soccer can be

ex_____ing and can be played whether you are a_____tic or not. Many

p_____le are not very g_____d players when they begin soccer, but end up b_____g

excellent players as they p_____ce.

Tennis is another f_____n game to learn. P_____s can play this s_____t for

many years, even as a_____s. Tennis skills include k_____ing your eye on the

b_____l and learning to r_____n quickly.

No matter w_____t sport you might ch_____se, playing games is f_____n and will

keep you h_____thy.

Choose the Definition

Directions: Read the passage, then choose the definition of each bold word from the choices below. If you do not know the meaning of a word, try using the choices in the passage to see what makes sense.

Jason and Jenny were working **diligently** on their school project. They had only two weeks to build a bridge of matchsticks that could **withstand** twenty pounds of weight. The two students worked every day after school and even **sacrificed** their weekend activities, missing games and movies, just to get their work done. When they turned in their completed project, the teacher said it was **exemplary** and gave them both A's on their work.

1. Diligently means
   a. lazily
   b. noisily
   c. persistently
   d. lovingly

2. Withstand means
   a. work
   b. survive
   c. be with
   d. sit on

3. Sacrificed means
   a. enjoyed
   b. gave up
   c. did not like
   d. participated

4. Exemplary means
   a. messy
   b. old
   c. excellent
   d. crazy

Quiz—Context Clues

1. What are context clues?

_____

_____

_____

_____

2. What are some words that help you find direct context clues?

_____

_____

_____

_____

3. What steps do you use to find the meaning of an unknown word in a sentence?

_____

_____

_____

_____

4. How do you know if a word is important enough to try to define?

_____

_____

_____

_____

Name: _____

Figure #13-5

Reading Connection Newsletter

Dear Parents/Guardians:

This week we learned about context clues. Sometimes as we read we come across a word we do not know. This week we learned strategies for figuring out the meaning of that word. First we must decide if the word is important enough to stop our reading to define it. If it is keeping us from understanding the text, then we have several things we can do. We can skip the word, read to the end of the sentence, and then go back to see if we can figure it out. We can substitute a word that makes sense in the sentence. We can look at the first and last sounds in the word to see what would be a logical word in that space. While reading, we also should say "blank" when we come across an unknown word, and frequently the right word will come to mind or we will see that the word isn't important to our comprehension and can be skipped for the time being.

Next week we will be working on predicting as we read. This is a concept that lends itself to fun activities and important information about how good readers read.

Please write the date next to each day.

Friday _____	Saturday _____	Sunday _____	Monday _____
Minutes read	Minutes read	Minutes read	Minutes read
_____	_____	_____	_____
Tuesday _____	Wednesday _____	Thursday _____	
Minutes read	Minutes read	Minutes read	
_____	_____	_____	

Student's name _____

Parent/Guardian signature _____ Date _____

Week 14—Predicting

Predicting involves using background knowledge and forethought to determine what might subsequently happen in text. By putting together the clues in the text, readers can guess what may happen next. Incorporating prior knowledge makes the prediction an educated guess. Predicting without using background knowledge is simply making a wild guess.

Good readers are constantly asking themselves what will happen next in what they are reading. Reading is the process of continually predicting and going back to check whether those predictions were right or wrong. When they are incorrect, readers must adjust their predictions to fit the new information they have found or the background knowledge they have used.

Prediction is an important strategy because it:

- gives readers an investment in the outcome of the text

- helps the reader see the connection between background knowledge and new information

- provides a purpose for reading

- keeps readers interested in the material

- encourages active reading

- provides a framework on which to attach new information and details

- helps readers anticipate meaning based on their knowledge of text structure, topic, context, and background knowledge

---

Prediction is used before, during, and after reading. Before reading, students preview the material, read the title, look at illustrations and questions, etc. They base their predictions on what they are observing plus their prior knowledge. During reading, students confirm or reject the predictions they have made based on the new knowledge they are receiving through the text. Rejected predictions can be replaced or revised at this time. After reading, students need to review and evaluate all predictions that were made before and during reading. If they were incorrect, what information was faulty? How could these errors be avoided in the future? Were any predictions simply wild guesses that were not based on prior knowledge?

Predictions can give focus and interest to reading at all levels. This is a strategy that is essential instruction in all grades and for all readers.

Lessons and Activities

1. Show the title and cover of an unfamiliar book to the class. Ask for student input as to the content of the book. What will it be about? What kinds of characters will there be? What action might you expect in this book? Explain that this is making predictions. Good readers make predictions constantly as they read. Go through the steps before, during, and after reading, using predictions as outlined above. Pass out copies of novels, making sure each student has an unfamiliar book. Ask them to preview the book and make predictions in writing. Discuss these as a class.

2. Display a list of vocabulary words from a novel the students are about to begin. Ask them to make up a story based on those words. Make sure the words include names, places, and actions. Save these and compare them to the book after reading is finished.

3. Figure #14-1 is an activity to be used before, during, and after reading. When beginning a new text, ask students to complete the correct row. Continue the chart during and after reading. When the book has been finished, go over the making and revision of predictions.

4. Practice making predictions by reading a sentence and writing what may happen next on Figure #14-2. Remind students to use their prior knowledge when doing this and beware of wild guesses.

5. Students are often fascinated by the concept of wild guesses. A fun activity is to write a simple statement, such as "The boy climbed the tree," on the board and let the students make up wild guesses about what might happen next. Make several examples of this. Students will each want a turn at the board to make their own silly, wild guesses.

6. Allow students to make predictions about what might happen in their own lives or in the world before the end of the school year. Put their written predictions in an envelope to be opened and read during the last week of school. **Note:** Put a message in your planbook to review these, or they may be found after school is out.

Novel Prediction Chart

Directions: This chart is to be used before, during, and after reading a novel. Next to "Before Reading," write what you think the book will be about when you preview the title, cover, and quickly look through the book. Next to "During Reading," write what you discover about your predictions as you read and make changes to your predictions. Finally, when you finish reading, write how your predictions and background knowledge helped you understand this book next to "After Reading."

1. Before Reading
2. During Reading
3. After Reading

Prediction Practice

Directions: Read each sentence. Use your background knowledge to help you predict what might happen next. Do not make wild guesses.

Event	**Prediction**
1. Sam went to a carnival.	_____
2. The sky got dark and cloudy.	_____
3. The batteries wore out.	_____
4. My cat went outside.	_____
5. I didn't do my homework.	_____
6. A car sped down the street.	_____
7. Joey was angry.	_____
8. The playground was hot.	_____
9. The lights went out.	_____
10. The class was noisy.	_____

Quiz—Predicting

1. What are predictions?

_____

_____

_____

2. Give an example of a good prediction.

_____

_____

_____

3. What are wild guesses?

_____

_____

_____

4. Give an example of a wild guess.

_____

_____

_____

5. What must you use in making good predictions?

_____

_____

_____

6. Make a prediction based on the information you have read so far in your class novel.

_____

_____

_____

Reading Connection Newsletter

Dear Parents/Guardians:

It is always fun to make predictions. But did you know that readers make predictions constantly as they read? What will happen next? What new characters might there be? How will this end? This week we learned that making predictions makes us more interested in what we are reading because we want to know if we will be right. We have to use our background knowledge when we predict, or we are just making wild guesses that don't make sense.

Next week we will be learning about the difference between fact and opinion and how that affects our reading. This is an important skill in becoming critical readers.

Please fill out the at-home reading log below and be sure to return the log Friday morning. Thank you.

Please write the date next to each day.

Friday _____	Saturday _____	Sunday _____	Monday _____
Minutes read	Minutes read	Minutes read	Minutes read
_____	_____	_____	_____
Tuesday _____	Wednesday _____	Thursday _____	
Minutes read	Minutes read	Minutes read	
_____	_____	_____	

Student's name _____

Parent/Guardian signature _____ Date _____

Week 15—Fact and Opinion

Critical readers must distinguish between fact and opinion in the text they read. This is especially crucial with young readers. Authors can advance their own ideologies and viewpoints through literature without young readers even knowing it is happening. They are apt to believe anything they see in print. Teachers have a great responsibility to teach students the difference between provable information and someone's point of view.

Much work needs to be done in finding the differences between fact and opinion in the grade 3–5 classroom. Constant modeling and questioning about this skill will make students aware of the ways beliefs can be disguised as the truth. In reading fiction, this is a relatively easy task. Students understand that fiction is "not true." Nonfiction, by its elementary definition, is true. Readers must understand that it must be a provable fact to be considered true.

Lessons and Activities

1. Read a factual news article to the students. Ask them how they can prove this material is true. What sources could they consult to prove the veracity of the text? Discuss how writers of newspaper articles must research and find verifiable sources for their work. Next, read a column from the Editorial Page that is understandable to students this age. Can these facts be proven? Is this just what the writer thinks? Might other people have different opinions? Use the terms fact and opinion in explaining this. Point out that everything that is read is either fact or opinion and that critical readers can differentiate between the two.

2. Figure #15-1 asks students to distinguish between fact and opinion in sentences. After doing this activity, divide students into small groups and let them compare answers. They must defend their work if there are disagreements amongst group members.

3. Give students practice in using fact and opinion by dividing the class into two groups. The groups are to consider the topic "School vacations should be longer." One group uses only facts to support the statement, one uses only opinions. Present the results and discuss the differences. Which was easier? Why?

4. Using materials in the classroom such as novels, magazines, nonfiction books, and newspapers, ask students to complete Figure #15-2.

5. As homework, ask students to listen to a newscast on television and take notes of one fact and one opinion presented. Was the opinion presented as fact, or did the speaker say it was his or her belief? Present in class tomorrow.

6. Prepare several index cards with topics printed on them such as "litter," "kindness to animals," etc. Ask pairs of students to share a card and present one fact and one opinion about the topic to the class. Allow class discussion of these topics.

7. If your school has a newspaper or newsletter, distribute copies to the students. Ask them to highlight in yellow the facts they can find and in another color, the opinions.

Fact or Opinion?

Directions: Read each sentence. Is it a fact or an opinion? Write F for fact or O for opinion on the line next to each sentence.

_____ Milk is good for your body.

_____ Dogs are the best pets.

_____ A cold is spread through germs.

_____ Everyone should be friendly to everyone else.

_____ Students must play a musical instrument.

_____ Boys are better at sports than girls.

_____ Girls are better at math than boys.

_____ The sun sets in the west.

_____ Many animals live in the ocean.

_____ Teachers are the smartest people in the school.

Fact and Opinion in Text

Directions: Using the written material in your classroom, find examples of fact and opinion. Write the title of what you have read and copy the statement. Then circle fact or opinion.

1. Title: _____

   Statement: _____

   _____

   _____

   This is (circle one):   fact   opinion

2. Title: _____

   Statement: _____

   _____

   _____

   This is (circle one):   fact   opinion

3. Title: _____

   Statement: _____

   _____

   _____

   This is (circle one):   fact   opinion

Quiz—Fact and Opinion

1. What is a fact?

   _____

   _____

   _____

2. What is an opinion?

   _____

   _____

   _____

3. Why is it important for readers to know the difference between fact and opinion?

   _____

   _____

   _____

4. Give an example of either a fact or an opinion you read in class this week. Prove that it is true or just someone's viewpoint.

   _____

   _____

   _____

Name: _____

Figure #15-4

Reading Connection Newsletter

Dear Parents/Guardians:

Students do not always discriminate between fact and opinion when they are reading. Authors have a great deal of power to influence young readers by putting their own viewpoint into work that students consider factual. Learning that not everything read is provable fact is an important concept for readers. This week we have done a lot of work determining fact and opinion. Parents/guardians need to listen to what students are reading and listening to on television. What is provable and what is one person's belief?

Next week we will learn about graphic reading. This is reading charts, pictures, graphs, and maps. These are very valuable tools to enrich comprehension. Be watching for homework, please.

Please continue to fill out the weekly at-home reading logs. This reading outside of school is essential in building good readers.

Please write the date next to each day.

Friday _____ Minutes read _____	Saturday _____ Minutes read _____	Sunday _____ Minutes read _____	Monday _____ Minutes read _____
Tuesday _____ Minutes read _____	Wednesday _____ Minutes read _____	Thursday _____ Minutes read _____	

Student's name _____

Parent/Guardian signature _____ Date _____

Week 16—Reading Graphics

Graphics simplify reading for information by the use of pictures, graphs, charts, and maps. The data is presented in a visual manner which allows for quicker access to the material. Good readers use graphics to make their understanding more effective and efficient.

Students in all grades can enjoy learning about and reading graphics. They will see how graphics make information easier to understand than reading paragraphs and pages of data. The use of many examples and plenty of modeling is part of the instruction of this concept, so teachers need to do an abundance of searching for articles, charts, maps, newspaper articles, and pictures before starting this unit of work. The children will also bring in examples of graphics, so the classroom will be a virtual exhibition area of graphic material.

Lessons and Activities

1. Make an overhead transparency of a chart or graph from the newspaper. Ask the students to tell you what information they learned from it. Is this easier than reading a whole article? Is this faster? Explain the concept of reading graphics. Ask for more examples. The students might not think about maps and photographs being graphics. Be sure to include line graphs, bar graphs, and pie charts. Explain that even unfamiliar topics such as the stock market can be read through the use of clues on the charts. Show a graph illustrating the ups and downs of the stock market. Do students have to know what stocks are to know if the market has gone up or down? **Note:** Using *USA Today* as a resource can be valuable. It is full of examples of graphics.

2. After the initial discussion of reading graphics, give a homework assignment to bring in an example of a graphic. Tell students to be prepared to show it to the class and discuss how it makes information easier to read.

3. Have a class discussion about how reading graphics is part of every class. Using math, social studies, and science books, ask students to complete Figure #16-1 telling about the use of charts, maps, etc., in their textbooks. Tell the students to look for a variety of examples.

4. Walk around the school and look for examples of graphics. There are pictures, maps, photos, charts, and graphs everywhere. Return to class and discuss.

5. Play a map game with the classroom wall map or individual atlases. If students have not had basic training in maps skills, explain the directions—north, south, east, and west. Then indicate where your school or town is on the map and ask for directions to various easily-found places on the map. If skills are in place, make the game harder with more difficult locations to place. Remind the students that maps are graphics.

6. Ask students to look at Figure #16-2. This is a chart of information about sports. Have them read the information and answer the questions. Then instruct the students to write a paragraph about the information on the chart. Which is easier to understand?

Reading Graphics in Textbooks

Directions: Using a math, social studies, or science textbook, find examples of graphics. Draw two of them below and write what you learned from them.

1. Drawing of graphic from my _____ textbook

This is what it tells me: _____

_____

_____

2. Drawing of graphic from my _____ textbook

This is what it tells me: _____

_____

_____

Reading a Chart

Directions: Read the chart below. Answer the questions. Then turn this page over and write what you learned from the chart in one paragraph.

Sports

Sport	Equipment	Season	Cost to play
Soccer	pads, ball, shoes, net	Fall, Spring, Summer	High
Baseball	ball, bat, helmet, shoes, pads	Fall, Spring	Low
Hockey	pads, stick, puck, helmet, net, skates	Winter	Very High

Which sport is most expensive? _____

Which sport requires the most equipment? _____

Which sport can you play in the summer? _____

Why is hockey not a summer sport? _____

Which sport costs the least to play? _____

Now write a paragraph on the back of this page about what you learned from the chart.

Quiz—Reading Graphics

1. What are graphics?

_____

_____

_____

2. Why is it helpful to understand how to read graphics?

_____

_____

_____

3. What are three examples of graphics?

a. _____

b. _____

c. _____

4. Give an example of a graphic in a textbook.

_____

_____

_____

5. Where did you find the graphic you brought to class as homework?

_____

_____

_____

Name: _____

Figure #16-4

Reading Connection Newsletter

Dear Parents/Guardians:

As good readers, we all need to know how to interpret information from charts, graphs, pictures, maps, and photographs. This reading is helpful in textbooks, newspapers, magazines, the Internet, and many other sources. This week we learned how to use graphics to make data easier to access and more efficient to work with. We found examples at home and in school and found that it was easier to use than having to read through pages of information. Please help us find examples at home when you are reading.

Next week we will be learning how to determine the importance of reading material. What is truly important for us to read and what is not as essential?

Please fill out the at-home reading log below and return to school Friday morning. Thank you.

Please write the date next to each day.

Friday _____ Minutes read _____	Saturday _____ Minutes read _____	Sunday _____ Minutes read _____	Monday _____ Minutes read _____
Tuesday _____ Minutes read _____	Wednesday _____ Minutes read _____	Thursday _____ Minutes read _____	

Student's name _____

Parent/Guardian signature _____ Date _____

Week 17—Determining Importance

Students must understand that there can be an abundance of information in nonfiction text, not all of which is necessary to comprehend the main idea. Interesting details can often sidetrack readers and guide them away from what they are really looking for. In teaching about determining importance, emphasize that setting a purpose for reading must come first. Without knowing why they are reading or what they are looking for, readers cannot understand what the most important points, information, or ideas are. All work on this strategy must be prefaced by setting a specific purpose for reading.

Determining importance is deciding and remembering what is the most important idea in the text. Students, mentally or physically, make lists of information gleaned from the text and prioritize. By previewing the material, students can find clues to determining importance. They must notice the features of text such as captions, bold print, italics, headings, illustrations, graphic reading, framed text, fonts, and clue words to determine what the author thought the main point should be. Authors often leave clues about what is important with words like "in summary," "most importantly," or "as a result."

> *In teaching about determining importance, emphasize that setting a purpose for reading must come first. Without knowing why they are reading or what they are looking for, readers cannot understand what the most important points, information, or ideas are.*

Determining importance is a vital strategy for all nonfiction reading. It provides a "hook" on which to hang the central knowledge of the text. It gives readers the most essential information in the reading material. It makes reading meaningful and assists in retaining key knowledge.

Lessons and Activities

1. Read a nonfiction passage to students. Be sure to talk about your purpose for reading this. ("Today I want to learn about what sharks eat, so I am going to read this article.") After reading the passage aloud, talk with the students about what the important information in the article was. Write their ideas on the board. Then go back to your stated purpose. Which important information really addressed the purpose? What told you what sharks eat? Which information on the board was very interesting but did not answer your questions? Explain that determining importance has everything to do with setting a purpose. Talk about prioritizing information. Write numbers next to each suggested idea and rank them in order of importance as determined by the purpose. Could you have done that without a purpose? Explain that different people make different choices when ranking importance because they may have different purposes.

2. Distribute and introduce a nonfiction text. Set a purpose for reading it by previewing the material. Each student may have a different purpose after looking over the text features outlined in the second paragraph of this chapter. Look at the book as a whole. What is the most important idea? Next, look at the book at the chapter level. Can students determine the importance of a specific chapter? Break this down even further. What is the most important word in a certain sentence? Ask students to respond to these questions in writing. Remind them to think about their stated purpose for reading the material. Make sure all answers from book level, to chapter level, to sentence level reflect this purpose.

3. Highlighting text is an activity elementary students may find entertaining. If children are taught the correct thinking that goes behind highlighting during these first experiences, they will use this as a valuable learning tool throughout school. The first impulse students have is to highlight everything. Explain that only the important ideas and information should be highlighted. Again, go back to purpose. Highlight only what matches the purpose for reading. There are many interesting facts and ideas in print, but they do not all reflect the reason for reading. Rather than highlighting these interesting ideas, students might be encouraged to put a star in the margin next to something they might want to re-read someday. Reserve the highlighter for purposeful information. Using Figure #17-1, ask the students to read the purpose and material, then go back and highlight the important parts. Then, at the bottom, they should justify their choices.

4. Learning about determining importance is vital in doing research for papers as the students get older. Begin the habit of taking notes while reading by asking children to complete Figure #17-2. They will use materials they are reading in class to find four important ideas or details after setting a purpose for reading. Next, they will write each of their important ideas in one of the boxes and illustrate it. They may cut these out and put them in correct sequence or in order of importance. By stapling them together, they have a mini-book that reduces the reading to four major ideas. This can be a first step in using notecards in future research.

Highlighting

Directions: The purpose for reading this text has been set for you. Read the material and highlight only the sentences that support your purpose. At the bottom of the page, explain why you highlighted those sentences.

Purpose: to find out where sharks live

   Sharks can be found in water all over the world. They are fish rather than mammals because they breathe through gills in their sides. Not all sharks are dangerous to people. They can be found in warm waters in the ocean, although some live in cold water. It seems that some sharks move to warmer waters at different times of the year. A few sharks live in rivers or bays connected to the ocean. Sharks' favorite food is fresh fish. The whale shark is the biggest shark. It can be 50 feet long and weigh 15 tons!

Why did you highlight the sentences you did? _____

_____

_____

_____

What interesting facts did not support your purpose for reading? _____

_____

_____

_____

Doing Research

Directions: Using the text you are reading in class, determine the purpose for reading. Then find four facts or ideas that support that purpose. Write one in each of the four boxes below and illustrate the information. Cut out the four boxes and put them in order of importance.

Fact #1: _____ _____ _____	Fact #2: _____ _____ _____
Fact #3: _____ _____ _____	Fact #4: _____ _____ _____

Quiz—Determining Importance

1. Why do good readers have to determine importance?

   _____

   _____

   _____

   _____

2. What must you do before you can determine importance?

   _____

   _____

   _____

   _____

3. What did you learn about highlighting material?

   _____

   _____

   _____

   _____

4. Name five clues authors give about what is important.

   a. _____

   b. _____

   c. _____

   d. _____

   e. _____

Name: _____

Figure #17-4

Reading Connection Newsletter

Dear Parents/Guardians:

This week we learned about determining importance in reading material. There is so much information in nonfiction reading that it is often difficult to understand what is truly important to know and remember and what can be read, but not classified as really essential. The major consideration for doing this is setting a purpose for reading. If we know why we are reading, we can look for the ideas, concepts, and information that support that reason. We practiced using highlighters in reading to indicate only the ideas that are important to our purpose.

Next week we will be learning about inference, which is "reading between the lines." We will find out how to determine what an author wants us to know, even if it is not written in black and white.

Thank you for filling out the at-home reading log and returning it each Friday morning.

Please write the date next to each day.

Friday _____ Minutes read _____	Saturday _____ Minutes read _____	Sunday _____ Minutes read _____	Monday _____ Minutes read _____
Tuesday _____ Minutes read _____	Wednesday _____ Minutes read _____	Thursday _____ Minutes read _____	

Student's name _____

Parent/Guardian signature _____ Date _____

Week 18—Inference and Drawing Conclusions

Inference is also called "reading between the lines." When readers use inference, they understand the author's meaning even if the words are not stated in the text. Readers use the author's words and their own background knowledge to draw a conclusion, or make an inference. Students can be taught to make an "addition problem" of this. They learn that "what I read" plus "what I already know" equals "an inference." Therefore, if they read "The clouds were dark and heavy," and they know that "Dark clouds mean rain," their inference is that it will rain.

Students can use the analogy that inference is detective work. The author has left clues that must be put together like a mystery. The author wants readers to make some connections on their own, so they have left some things unwritten and given the reader credit for figuring them out. Inference means reading the clues and making a good guess based on prior knowledge. Clues are put together with background knowledge, and a new concept is developed.

Note: There are some students who will have difficulty with this concept. Small "needs groups" often work well when developing the concept of inference. Beginning with short riddles and building up to work in the class text is necessary for these students.

What I Read + What I Already Know = Inference

Lessons and Activities

1. Introduce the concept of drawing conclusions and making inferences by using a simple riddle. "I am red. I grow on a tree. I have a stem and leaves. You can make pies and sauce with me." The answer is apples. How did students know that? Did anyone say cherries? What clue narrowed the topic down to apples? (sauce) Explain that the students took what they read (all the clues) and put them together with their background knowledge to draw a conclusion or make an inference.

2. Distribute Figure #18-1. Instruct students to read the story and use the inference addition problem to draw conclusions.

3. Ask students to write riddles to draw conclusions like the ones in Activity #1. Use these riddles as bell-starters at the beginning of class each day or as "sponge" activities when lessons have finished early. Make sure the author of each riddle gets credit for his/her work.

4. There are many commercially-produced books with short mysteries for children. Some are workbooks with stories to read and questions to answer that call for inferential thinking. Others are simply short mysteries which can be read in one sitting. Either type is excellent for supporting this unit of study. Read the mystery aloud and ask for the conclusions and inferences the children have drawn. Discuss what background knowledge they used to figure out their theories.

5. Distribute Figure #18-2 and ask students to use the material they are reading in class to complete the chart about making inferences. This makes the concept relevant to current work.

Drawing Conclusions

Directions: Using the inference addition problem, What I Read + What I Already Know = Inference, read the following story, complete the Inference Organizer below, and answer the question about inference.

Bailey was a small, furry, gray cat. He was always finding some kind of trouble to make in the Smith house. He tore apart newspapers and scratched the furniture. Sometimes, Mrs. Smith wanted to give him away! One night as the family was sleeping, Bailey began screeching and scratching at the bedroom doors. He made so much noise that the family woke up and found that they had to go outside immediately. Bailey had saved their lives! Mrs. Smith never wanted to give him away again.

Inference Organizer

What I Read	+	What I Already Know	=	Inference

What made Bailey act the way he did?

_____

_____

_____

_____

Making Inferences

Directions: Use this Inference Organizer with the book you are reading in class to determine what the author expects you to think. Remember to use your background knowledge with what you read to make an inference.

Title of book: _____

Inference Organizer

What I Read +	What I Already Know =	Inference

What did the author expect you to already know? _____

_____

Could you have understood the text without your background knowledge?

_____

Quiz—Inference and Drawing Conclusions

1. What is an inference?

   _____

   _____

   _____

2. What must you use to make an inference?

   _____

   _____

   _____

3. Draw an Inference Organizer (or addition problem).

4. Why do good readers make inferences?

   _____

   _____

   _____

5. Why do authors use inferences?

   _____

   _____

   _____

Name: _____

Figure #18-4

Reading Connection Newsletter

Dear Parents/Guardians:

   This week we learned about drawing conclusions and making inferences. Many times authors do not write everything they want the reader to know. They assume that the reader can read "beyond the text" or "between the lines." Good readers add their own background knowledge to what they are reading to understand what the author is saying. We practiced with riddles and our textbooks to find the meaning by adding our prior knowledge to our reading.

   Next week we will be learning about recognizing complete sentences. This will help our reading and our writing skills.

   Please fill out the at-home reading log below and return it to class on Friday morning. The students who are doing the most at-home reading have a real advantage in developing their reading skills. Thank you.

Please write the date next to each day.

Friday _____ Minutes read _____	Saturday _____ Minutes read _____	Sunday _____ Minutes read _____	Monday _____ Minutes read _____
Tuesday _____ Minutes read _____	Wednesday _____ Minutes read _____	Thursday _____ Minutes read _____	

Student's name _____

Parent/Guardian signature _____ Date _____

Week 19—Recognizing Complete Sentences

Understanding complete sentences, parts of sentences, punctuation, and capitalization is important to becoming a good reader. Punctuation and capitalization give very important clues to reading sentences and understanding words.

Although students may have been exposed to the elements of sentences in previous grades, this is a good time to make sure they are all understood. Teaching what is a subject, a predicate, and a modifier will help develop the basis of sentences. A subject is who or what the sentence is about. Subjects are nouns or pronouns and their modifiers. A predicate is the action of that subject. Predicates are verbs and their modifiers. Additionally, all complete sentences must stand on their own.

Capitalization is an essential skill that has most likely been taught since kindergarten. A refresher lesson on when to use capital letters is important at every grade level. Students at upper grades are known to print everything in capital letters because they aren't sure when to use them and when not. In teaching about sentences, the important capital letter is the one at the beginning of the sentence. This shows where the sentence starts. Punctuation is equally important because the final punctuation shows where the sentence ends and gives a clue as to what kind of sentence it might be. The four types of sentences are: declarative (makes a statement), interrogative (asks a question), imperative (gives a command), and exclamatory (makes an exclamation). The punctuation is a clue to the type of sentence with declarative having a period at the end, interrogative having a question mark, and exclamatory having an exclamation point. Imperative may have either a period or exclamation point.

Lessons and Activities

1. After initial instruction of the parts of complete sentences, write one word on the board. The more interesting the word, the better. Discuss what part of a sentence it would be, subject or predicate. Ask each student to write a complete sentence using that word. The next step is to write two words on the board and, again, write a sentence using those words.

2. Figure #19-1 is an activity on which students will identify the subject and the predicate for a number of sentences. This is also a good assessment tool for teachers, as it indicates strengths and weaknesses in this concept.

3. Cut headlines out of newspapers. These are excellent examples of incomplete sentences. Ask students to decide what is missing from each and make them complete sentences.

4. Review the necessary components of complete sentences. Remind the students that each sentence must have a subject and a predicate and must be able to stand on its own and make sense. Using Figure #19-2, instruct students to determine whether sentences are complete or incomplete.

5. Take a walk around the school. When you return to the classroom, have each student write five complete sentences about what he/she observed. Additionally, on the walk, ask them to look for signs of incomplete sentences around the building.

6. Pass out books in which students will look for examples of the four kinds of sentences. Allow them to come up to the board to write their sentences under labels of declarative, interrogative, imperative, and exclamatory.

Parts of a Sentence

Directions: Read each of the sentences below. Write the subject and predicate for each sentence in the spaces provided.

Sentence	Subject	Predicate
1. Dogs are animals.		
2. The day turned cloudy and dark.		
3. Swimming is more fun in the ocean.		
4. Tim collects model trains.		
5. Are you going to the movie?		
6. Boys, stop that noise!		
7. When the sun shines, I get a tan.		
8. Mark fell off his skateboard.		
9. Cars are not built to last forever.		
10. Singing in the choir is fun.		

Is This Complete?

Directions: Read each sentence below. On the line before the sentence write C for Complete Sentence or I for Incomplete Sentence. Make sure each complete sentence has a subject and predicate and makes sense by itself.

1. _____ As the girls shopped in the mall.

2. _____ The dolphin jumped into the air.

3. _____ The sunny, bright day.

4. _____ She skipped happily down the road.

5. _____ The very, very hard test.

6. _____ Going to the beach for summer vacation.

7. _____ Climbing up the tallest mountain in the country.

8. _____ She didn't know.

9. _____ Birds sing.

10. _____ Happily ever after.

Quiz—Recognizing Complete Sentences

1. What two parts must a complete sentence have?

   _____

   _____

   _____

2. What must a complete sentence do?

   _____

   _____

   _____

3. What are the four types of sentences?

   a. _____

   b. _____

   c. _____

   d. _____

4. Give an example of a complete sentence.

   _____

   _____

   _____

5. Give an example of an incomplete sentence.

   _____

   _____

   _____

Name: _____

Figure #19-4

Reading Connection Newsletter

Dear Parents/Guardians:

   This week we have learned about complete sentences. There are many concepts used in learning this. First, we learned about subjects and predicates. Next, we learned about the four types of sentences: declarative (makes a statement), interrogative (asks a question), imperative (gives a command), and exclamatory (makes an exclamation). We also reviewed capital letters and punctuation because they show the beginning and end of sentences.

   Next week we will learn about reading for different purposes. We will discuss reading for information, meaning, and enjoyment.

   Thank you for completing the at-home reading log again this week. By now you must be hearing more fluent reading and recognizing better comprehension than at the beginning of the school year. Please remember to return this form to school on Friday morning.

Please write the date next to each day.

Friday _____	Saturday _____	Sunday _____	Monday _____
Minutes read	Minutes read	Minutes read	Minutes read
_____	_____	_____	_____
Tuesday _____	Wednesday _____	Thursday _____	
Minutes read	Minutes read	Minutes read	
_____	_____	_____	

Student's name _____

Parent/Guardian signature _____ Date _____

Week 20—Reading for Different Purposes

Students need to understand that their purpose for reading affects how carefully they read and their rate of reading. Up until third grade, students are "learning to read." From this point on, the focus in many classes becomes "reading to learn." Therefore, the purpose set for each reading of text becomes even more important. Students become aware that reading the comics and reading a science textbook are two very different types of tasks read with differing amounts of attention to detail and at differing speeds. In teaching the concept of reading for a variety of purposes, the main question that must be answered is "Why am I reading this?"

The three major reasons for reading are for information, meaning, and enjoyment. One of the major differences in the various ways of reading for these diverse purposes is that stories that are read for enjoyment are read from the beginning straight through to the end. In reading for information, it is all right to skip from one part of the material to another to find the facts and ideas the reader is seeking.

Another difference in reading for varied purposes is the rate of reading. Many children come into reading classes with the single purpose of wanting to read faster. All students need to understand that reading fast is not necessarily reading well. The purpose for reading can determine the rate. Skimming through a light novel or magazine article is much faster than reading a biography or a text about natural disasters. Practice in determining reasons for reading is necessary to determine speed of reading.

Lessons and Activities

1. Using a wide variety of materials such as novels, textbooks, newspapers, Internet articles, comics, tests, advertisements, magazines, class handouts, reference books, letters, e-mails, overhead transparencies, and empty medicine bottles, ask students to suggest reasons for reading each item. Write the purposes they come up with on the board. Are they read for enjoyment, safety, directions, avoidance of boredom, or as an assignment? What other reasons can they suggest? Next, ask how each would be read. Let the students separate the texts into categories. Which would be read quickly and without much attention to detail? Which would take a long time to read and might have to be re-read? About which ones will the students have to answer questions after reading? Explain that all reading has a purpose and that purpose varies from text to text.

2. Ask students what they have read today. List on the board all the answers. They may have read the cereal box at breakfast, the side of the school bus, the comics in the paper, instructions in class, the bell-starter, or the menu in the cafeteria. Next to what they have read, write what their purpose was. Hand out Figure #20-1 and explain that they must list everything they read for 24 hours beginning right now. They will take the paper home and keep track there also, bringing back the paper in the morning and continuing until this time tomorrow. In addition to what they read, the worksheet asks why they read. Explain that the entire form must be completed. The back of the paper or additional sheets may be used.

3. What happens if a purpose is not set? Ask students to list the consequences of not having a purpose for reading. "Surfing" the Internet is a result of not having a reason for reading on the Internet. How many more can the students think of?

4. Figure #20-2 is an opportunity to compare reading materials, purpose, and rate. Completing this raises awareness of the variety of texts and purposes students encounter.

24 Hours in My Reading Life

Directions: Keep track of everything you read in 24 hours on this chart. You will start this in class, take it home with you, and finish 24 hours later in class. Do not overlook anything. Even something as small as the "hot" and "cold" words on the faucet should be counted. Then, write what your purpose for reading those things might be. Did you read for enjoyment, safety, information, or some other reason? Use more paper if you need it.

What I Read	My Purpose for Reading
_____	_____
_____	_____
_____	_____
_____	_____
_____	_____
_____	_____
_____	_____
_____	_____
_____	_____
_____	_____
_____	_____
_____	_____
_____	_____

 ··· *POWer Strategies™ for Reading Comprehension Grades 3–5*

Reading for Different Purposes

Directions: Compare the texts you are reading now. What is your purpose for reading them? Is your reading speed fast, medium, or slow? Complete the lines below to see how differently you read with different materials.

1. Title of a novel you are reading: _____

   Purpose for reading: _____

   Speed of reading (circle one): fast   medium   slow

2. Title of your math book: _____

   Purpose for reading: _____

   Speed of reading (circle one):   fast   medium   slow

3. Name of a newspaper or magazine you read: _____

   Purpose for reading: _____

   Speed of reading (circle one):   fast   medium   slow

4. What have you read for directions? _____

   Purpose for reading: _____

   Speed of reading (circle one):   fast   medium   slow

Quiz—Reading for Different Purposes

1. Why do you need to have a purpose for reading?

   _____

   _____

   _____

2. What are four purposes you might have for reading?

   a. _____

   b. _____

   c. _____

   d. _____

3. If you do not set a purpose for reading while on the Internet, what might happen?

   _____

   _____

   _____

4. If you do not set a purpose for reading novels and textbooks, what might happen?

   _____

   _____

   _____

5. How does purpose determine the speed you read text?

   _____

   _____

   _____

Name: _____

Figure #20-4

Reading Connection Newsletter

Dear Parents/Guardians:

As good readers, we all set a purpose for reading. These purposes vary from one type of material to another. They determine how carefully we read and our reading speed. This week we carefully investigated the types of text we read and then looked at our attention to detail and speed. One interesting activity we did was keeping track of everything we read for 24 hours and why.

Next week we will be learning about informational text. This includes reference materials, newspapers, the Internet, and magazines.

Please continue to fill out the weekly at-home reading log. Thank you for supporting our reading in this way.

Please write the date next to each day.

Friday _____ Minutes read _____	Saturday _____ Minutes read _____	Sunday _____ Minutes read _____	Monday _____ Minutes read _____
Tuesday _____ Minutes read _____	Wednesday _____ Minutes read _____	Thursday _____ Minutes read _____	

Student's name _____

Parent/Guardian signature _____ Date _____

Week 21—Reading Informational Texts

Reading at third grade and above is primarily expository rather than narrative. Many commercial reading programs now include nonfiction in their basal textbooks, as well as the more common narrative or fiction material. Besides textbooks, students need to be able to work with reference materials on a daily basis. Learning how to recognize the contents of reference sources and which to use for specific purposes is an important skill all students should acquire.

The resources singled out for instruction are the almanac, Internet, encyclopedia, thesaurus, dictionary, and atlas. There are many others, as a trip to the Media Center will demonstrate. Introducing students to these materials is essential to their being able to take advantage of these valuable stores of knowledge.

Lessons and Activities

1. Introduce the concept of reference materials. Explain that they are full of information, facts, figures, and other material students might need to know, in an easy-to-use format. Have examples on hand. Go over each book and ask students if they have ever used these materials before. How did they use them? Were they helpful?

2. Take a trip to the Media Center. **Note:** Be sure you have told the librarian that you are coming to use the reference materials. Walk the students through the materials that are available for their use. Distribute Figure #21-1, requiring students to find the appropriate resource to answer questions. Before returning to class, discuss these forms.

3. Dictionary usage is a skill that all students need to have. Even though spell-checking programs assist when they are writing on the computer, knowledge of dictionaries is basic to all reading and writing. Figure #21-2 provides practice in using guide words to find entries in a dictionary.

4. On the board, write a topic for a research paper. Make this topic interesting to all students, such as natural disasters, Disney World, space travel, hobbies, wild animals, television, etc. Then obtain students' ideas for essential questions to be answered in a research paper about the topic. Write three or four of these questions on the board under the subject. Next, ask students to spend class time for one or two class periods (or assign homework) finding information to answer these questions. Model using notecards to write the information and material used as a resource. In the subsequent class period, put together all of the material students have found. Again, model how to organize the cards into similar categories and read all the material to write a paragraph about that question. This is the first step in learning how to write a research paper, and it is excellent practice in using informational material.

A follow-up lesson might include students researching and writing their own one-page paper about a topic in which they are interested. The important point is for them to document the resources they used.

5. The Internet has become the major source of information for much of the world. Reading on the Internet is a skill that students must master. There are some basic points that all students must understand: not all sources on the Internet are reliable; secondary sources to support an opinion or "fact" must be found; Internet reading must be done with a solid purpose in mind to avoid just "surfing" and wasting time. Depending on your school's policy for using the Internet and the availability of computers, a session devoted to finding information using this valuable resource can be conducted. This is an excellent lesson to use when building background knowledge or schema for a novel unit.

Media Center Scavenger Hunt

Directions: After the class introduction to reference materials in the library, find the answers to the following questions. Be sure to write where you found the information.

Question	Answer	Source
1. How many oceans are there in the world?	_____	_____
2. How do you say "Hello" in French?	_____	_____
3. What animals live in Australia?	_____	_____
4. On what day of the week was October 28, 1946?	_____	_____
5. What is another word for "enormous"?	_____	_____
6. Where was the largest earthquake ever recorded?	_____	_____
7. Who was the U.S. President in 1925?	_____	_____

Dictionary Search

Directions: In the box below are guide words and page numbers for a dictionary. In the chart, write the page number on which each word could be found in this dictionary.

merit–mesh	page 720	private–probable	page 916
greet–grill	page 505	equator–equipment	page 386
left–leg	page 656	staff–stain	page 1,132
cent–chain	page 183	cay–celery	page 179

Word	Found on page
legal	_____
grid	_____
chaff	_____
prize	_____
equipment	_____
merry	_____
stagger	_____
cellar	_____

 ⋯ *POWer Strategies™ for Reading Comprehension Grades 3–5*

Quiz—Reading Informational Texts

1. What is informational text?

   _____

   _____

   _____

   _____

2. Give five examples of informational texts.

   a. _____

   b. _____

   c. _____

   d. _____

   e. _____

3. Where would you find information about the largest tornado in U.S. history?

   _____

   _____

   _____

4. What steps did you learn about writing a research paper?

   a. _____

   b. _____

   c. _____

   d. _____

Reading Connection Newsletter

Dear Parents/Guardians:

   Using reference materials, or informational text, is an essential skill for all readers. We all use dictionaries, atlases, encyclopedias, the Internet, and many other sources to find information we need to know. This week, we practiced using all of these sources and more. We visited the Media Center and found the wealth of materials there for us to use. We learned some rules for using the Internet, such as checking that the source of information is reliable. What we learned about informational text this week is something we will use for the rest of our lives.

   Next week we will learn about story elements such as characters, setting, plot, genre, and point of view.

   Please be sure to fill out the at-home reading log at the bottom of this page with the date next to each day and the number of minutes read at home. Remember that this reading can be out loud or silent. If the reading is alone and silent, it is a good idea to ask questions about the material to make sure it was read and understood. Thank you.

Please write the date next to each day.

Friday _____ Minutes read _____	Saturday _____ Minutes read _____	Sunday _____ Minutes read _____	Monday _____ Minutes read _____
Tuesday _____ Minutes read _____	Wednesday _____ Minutes read _____	Thursday _____ Minutes read _____	

Student's name _____

Parent/Guardian signature _____ Date _____

Week 22—Story Elements

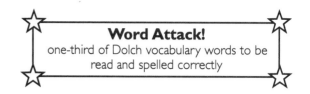
Although there are many differing opinions about what exactly are story elements, students in third through fifth grade need to learn only the very basic ones. Characters, setting, plot, genre, and point of view are the essential elements for students in these grades. Later they will be exposed to theme, purpose, symbolism, and others. In Chapter 23 genre will be discussed, and Chapter 25 covers point of view. In this chapter the elements of character, setting, and plot will be discussed.

It is hard to imagine reading literature without understanding the characters. Students tend to identify with well-written characters such as Opal in *Because of Winn-Dixie* or Ramona in the Beverly Cleary books. The study of characters is fun and brings out enjoyment in reading.

The setting is not only the place, but the time the book takes place. Much of the visualization that readers do is based on setting. Students must also learn that there is background knowledge that goes into understanding setting. Schema must be developed before reading to truly experience the book.

Plot is how the story plays out. What is the problem? How is it solved? What action takes place? Plot is interwoven with characters and setting. The characters are experiencing the plot in the time and place of the setting. Without all three of these elements, fiction would not make sense.

Lessons and Activities

1. Introduce and discuss characters, setting, and plot. Write these three words on the board and let students give examples. Explain that the wide variety of examples shows how important these elements are. Ask students to imagine books without characters, setting, or a plot. How interesting would they be?

2. Break the class into groups of 3 or 4. Ask them to write a short story (1 page) that incorporates all three of the elements they have learned. Share the stories aloud in class. This is really enjoyable if the groups are all given the same basic storyline, such as "A flying saucer landed on the school grounds."

3. Distribute Figure #22-1. Explain that students are to think of two different fairy tales or folk tales. Ask them to fill in information about characters, setting, and plot for each, comparing and contrasting.

4. Use the current read-aloud novel or group novels being used in class to complete Figure #22-2. What are the important characters, main setting (time and place), and plot (problem, solution, action) of the book? At the bottom of the page, instruct students to write what other things they would like to learn about those elements before they finish the book.

5. Write letters to characters in books. These may be postcards, e-mails, or letters. Students should refer to the plot as they write, asking the characters specific questions about what is happening in the book.

6. Make acrostic poems for book characters. Write a character's name down the side of the paper. Use each letter in the name as the first letter in a line of poetry about that character. Draw illustrations to go with the poems and display in the classroom.

7. Have a Character Talk Show. With one student as the host, three other students play the parts of characters from different novels (or the same novel). They have a discussion about things that are happening to them or answer general questions in the persona of their characters.

Figure #22-1

Story Elements Compare/Contrast

Directions: Think of two fairy tales or folk tales you have read. Write about their characters, setting, and plot. Compare and contrast the two stories.

Title	Characters	Setting	Plot
1.			
2.			

What elements are similar?

What elements are different?

Elements of Fiction

Directions: Using the novel you are reading in class, think of the characters, setting, and plot. Write about them below. Then, at the bottom of the page, write what you would like to know more about before you finish reading this book.

Title of book: _____

Author: _____

Characters:

_____

_____

Setting:

_____

_____

Plot:

_____

_____

What I would like to know about the characters:

_____

_____

What I would like to know about the setting:

_____

_____

What I would like to know about the plot:

_____

_____

Quiz—Story Elements

1. What 3 story elements did you learn about this week?

   a. _____

   b. _____

   c. _____

2. What does the first element tell about?

   _____

   _____

3. What does the second element tell about?

   _____

   _____

4. What does the third element tell about?

   _____

   _____

5. Why is it important for a story to have all three of these elements?

   _____

   _____

6. Who is your favorite character in a story? Why?

   _____

   _____

7. Tell about the plot of the book you are reading right now.

   _____

   _____

Name: _____

Figure #22-4

Reading Connection Newsletter

Dear Parents/Guardians:

Every story has many elements in common with other stories. This week we learned three of those elements: characters, setting, and plot. Using favorite old stories and our current novels in class, we practiced identifying and exploring these parts of fiction. We had a lot of fun with activities involving characters. We learned that setting is not only the place, but also when the story took place. Plot is the action, the problem, and the solution in the story.

Next week we will discuss the wide range of genres available. Introducing students to a broad selection of materials can improve their reading and writing skills.

Please fill out the weekly at-home reading form below. Be sure to discuss characters, setting, and plot during reading time. Thank you for your help.

Please write the date next to each day.

Friday _____ Minutes read _____	Saturday _____ Minutes read _____	Sunday _____ Minutes read _____	Monday _____ Minutes read _____
Tuesday _____ Minutes read _____	Wednesday _____ Minutes read _____	Thursday _____ Minutes read _____	

Student's name _____

Parent/Guardian signature _____ Date _____

Week 23—Genre

Teachers want their students to be exposed to a wide range of reading genres and to become immersed in the variety of text available for their information and interest. Introducing students to the broad selection of material they can read not only improves reading skills, but writing as well. As students learn about mystery, biography, and so forth, they should be encouraged to try writing in that style. Genre is also an excellent tool for integrating content subjects into language arts. A biography of an interesting person in history or a historical novel about a specific era being studied in social studies can make reading become an integral part of that class. Science fiction or technology materials can further the study of, and add interest to, science.

Reading classes become exciting places when a variety of material and genres are available. Teaching about these types of text is an important part of literacy instruction. Beginning with fiction and nonfiction as basic genres, the sub-genres multiply as students brainstorm ideas.

Lessons and Activities

1. Introduce the concept of genre. Ask students to list as many different genres as possible on the board or overhead projector. Some of the most common answers will be mystery (solving a crime or puzzle), realistic fiction (modern-day setting, could actually happen), science fiction (usually in future, elements of science or technology), historical fiction (set in history, partially historically accurate), folk or fairy tales, fantasy (not realistic, talking animals, etc.), humorous stories, short stories, poetry, plays, myths and legends, informational text, biographies, autobiographies, and letters and diaries. Keep this list as a chart posted near the classroom library for students' reference as they choose materials to read.

2. Visit the Media Center or school library. Using Figure #23-1, direct students to find as many genres of books as they can. See if they can figure out library organizational tools to help with this task, such as labels on book spines, signs over shelves, etc. After returning to the classroom, have a discussion about the variety of books available. Add to the chart by the classroom library. Poll the students to discover which genre is the most popular. Which is read most by girls? by boys? Which has not been read much by anyone in the class? What genres would students like to have in the classroom?

3. Conduct a classroom contest to design genre stickers to put on the books on the shelves. Which genres should be designated in this way? Then, make producing these labels for the spines of books a "free time" activity. If a magnifying glass, for instance, is chosen for mysteries, the mystery books on the shelves can be easily found by looking for the correct sticker. There may be many books without specific genres for which a sticker cannot be determined. In those instances, an interesting class discussion could evolve to decide why this is the case. Is the book a combination of genres? Is this a new genre that needs to be added to the class list?

4. Ask students to choose a folk or fairy tale they especially like. Direct them to write this tale on Figure #23-2 in a different genre. *The Three Bears* could become a mystery tale with the bears trying to put together clues to discover who broke into their house. "Paul Bunyan" could take place on an undiscovered planet in the future in a science fiction story. Allow students to refer to the chart of genres for inspiration for their writing.

Library Genre Search

Directions: On a trip to the Media Center or library, find as many different genres as possible. Write the title of the book and the genre on the lines below. Use the back of this page for additional books. We will discuss these lists when we return to class.

Title	Genre
1. _____	_____
2. _____	_____
3. _____	_____
4. _____	_____
5. _____	_____
6. _____	_____
7. _____	_____
8. _____	_____

Transformed Tales

Directions: Think of your favorite fairy tale or folk tale. Now imagine it as another genre. What if *Cinderella* were written as an autobiography or *The Three Little Pigs* became a science fiction story? This is your opportunity to have fun changing the genre of a story to make it different and interesting. Write your story below and be prepared to share it with the class. Use extra paper, if necessary.

_____

_____

_____

_____

_____

_____

_____

_____

_____

_____

_____

_____

_____

_____

_____

_____

_____

Quiz—Genre

1. What is genre?

_____

_____

_____

2. Write the names of six genres.

   a. _____

   b. _____

   c. _____

   d. _____

   e. _____

   f. _____

3. What is your favorite genre, and why?

_____

_____

_____

4. Write the titles of three books and identify the genre of each.

Title	Genre
a. _____	_____
b. _____	_____
c. _____	_____

Name: _____   Figure #23-4

Reading Connection Newsletter

Dear Parents/Guardians:

Genre is the type of writing used in text. For example, mystery, biography, science fiction, and poetry are all genres. This week we discovered the vast numbers of genre available in our classroom and the school library. We classified books and labeled them to indicate their genre and make them easy to find. We practiced writing using different genres. Please share your favorite genre while reading with your child. It is very interesting for students to know what other people like to read.

Next week we will be working on following written directions.

Please be sure to keep up the at-home reading. This week be sure to check that a variety of genres are being covered. It might be time to suggest some nonfiction reading for a child who is only reading novels or some fiction for those who seem only to read informational material. Thank you for your support of literacy at home.

Please write the date next to each day.

Friday _____	Saturday _____	Sunday _____	Monday _____
Minutes read	Minutes read	Minutes read	Minutes read
_____	_____	_____	_____
Tuesday _____	Wednesday _____	Thursday _____	
Minutes read	Minutes read	Minutes read	
_____	_____	_____	

Student's name _____

Parent/Guardian signature _____ Date _____

Week 24—Following Written Directions

How can a student survive school without skills in following written directions? It would be impossible. These skills do not come naturally, however. Sometimes teachers assume that because the instructions are written on the paper or in the book and because the students can read, they automatically can follow those directions. This is not always the case. Often, students read and comprehend instructions, but are not sure how to begin or follow through with the required work. Instructions in following written directions are essential at every grade level. As work becomes more difficult, guidelines become harder to follow and guidance should be given as needed.

The following lessons and activities begin at relatively easy levels of instruction and can be modified, as necessary, to match work levels being done in class. This is not just a one-time unit of study, but must be referred to over and over as the year progresses and different formats and sorts of directions must be followed.

The best way to model or teach the important skill of reading directions is with practical, hands-on, and relevant materials such as those used in class. Practice in writing their own directions gives students valuable tools for understanding reading other writers' directions.

Lessons and Activities

1. Conduct a classroom discussion about following written directions. Ask the students to go on a "hunt" in the room to find as many such directions as they can and write them down. When all children have returned to their seats, write their findings on the board. Discuss the variety and range of directions they found. Make sure things like fire drill and other safety procedures are listed. Discuss the importance of reading and following directions correctly.

2. Walk around the building looking for written directions. **Note:** Supply each child with a clipboard, if possible. This will make walking and writing simultaneously easier. Come back and compare notes. Why were all these directions important to have posted? Were they for safety, convenience, or information? What written directions would be helpful that are not posted in the building?

3. Figure #24-1 directs students to read specific directions and then color a picture on the paper. Look for students who focus on only the general directions and not details. Are these the same students who have difficulty on daily worksheets or in retelling or summarizing what they have read?

4. Put a list of directions you have written on an overhead projector. Ask students to follow those directions. Make this a fun activity. Add instructions such as "moo like a cow" and "stand on one foot with your hand on your head."

5. A very enjoyable activity for all students is getting the opportunity to design their own fast-food product. This might be a special food they like but cannot find at fast-food outlets. It might be a parent's specialty food that the student would like everyone to have. Figure #24-2 is a four-part worksheet on which their great idea can be designed while following the written directions.

6. Ask each student to think of something he/she is good at doing. Then have them each write directions for doing that. Share in small groups. Ask group members to comment on steps that might have been omitted. Encourage positive feedback in the groups.

Follow the Written Directions

Directions: Read the following directions carefully. Then, using crayons, markers, or colored pencils, illustrate what you are asked to draw.

Draw a large, blue, two-story house with brown steps leading up to the front door. Make five windows and two doors on the front of the house. There is a red flower pot in one window. Smoke is coming out of the chimney. A big apple tree is in the front yard. A squirrel is in the tree. Draw a bicycle on the lawn and a boy and a girl standing near it. A lady is on the front porch. On the left side of the paper, draw a green car sitting next to the house. Add any other details you want to make.

My Fast-Food Creation

Directions: Follow the directions in each box and develop your own fast-food product. Make this something you would want to buy and eat.

1. Name your product.	2. List the ingredients (What is in this food).
3. Write an ad for your product.	4. Draw a container for your food.

Quiz—Following Written Directions

1. Why is it important to know how to follow written directions?

   _____

   _____

   _____

   _____

2. Give two examples of written directions that are important to your safety.

   a. _____

   b. _____

3. Write complete directions for making a peanut butter sandwich. Do not leave out any steps. Make sure someone could read this and make a good sandwich.

   _____

   _____

   _____

   _____

   _____

   _____

   _____

   _____

   _____

Name: _____

Figure #24-4

Reading Connection Newsletter

Dear Parents/Guardians:

Following written directions is something that we all have to do every day. Think of all the directions you follow daily. You read street signs, recipes, safety notices, work-related directions, etc. This week we explored the many examples of reading directions at school. Students wrote their own directions for doing something they are good at doing. We found examples of written directions all over the school. Knowing how to read directions and look for important details in them is an essential skill.

Next week we will be learning about identifying the speaker in writing and finding the point of view in text.

Remember the at-home reading log below. These need to be returned to school, finished or unfinished, each Friday for credit. Thanks for your help.

Please write the date next to each day.

Friday _____	Saturday _____	Sunday _____	Monday _____
Minutes read	Minutes read	Minutes read	Minutes read
_____	_____	_____	_____
Tuesday _____	Wednesday _____	Thursday _____	
Minutes read	Minutes read	Minutes read	
_____	_____	_____	

Student's name _____

Parent/Guardian signature _____ Date _____

Week 25—Point of View

Word Attack!
synonyms

A major source of confusion and loss of comprehension comes from not understanding point of view in text. Readers may not know who is "telling the story," therefore not catching the nuances inherent in one person's feelings or viewpoint. As readers mature and their reading material becomes more varied, it is also important to understand that everything is written from the author's perspective. The editorial pages of the newspaper are written very differently from an encyclopedia entry. By interjecting feelings, opinions, biases, etc., writers can make their stories interesting, but students need to understand that what is being read is that person's view of the world.

Young readers often feel that anything in print must be unbiased. They must comprehend differing points of view. The easiest way to approach this concept is through "who is talking." By asking this, teachers make readers aware of the point of view. The signal words in a novel are "I," "me," "my," "we," and "our" for first person. Students know that they are reading the story through the words of someone who is actually in the story. Their next task, of course, is to identify who that person might be. The signal words "he," "she," "they," and "their" indicate third person, a narrator or storyteller who is outside of the story looking in. Students can relate to this in stories they have written about things they have not experienced first-hand.

Lessons and Activities

1. Read a traditional version of *The Three Little Pigs* to the class. Then read *The True Story of the Three Little Pigs* by Jon Scieszka, which is written from the wolf's point of view. Ask the students to identify the differences in the stories. Which portrayed the pigs as the protagonists (good guys)? Which made the wolf sound like the innocent party? How did the students visualize the characters in each book? Were there differences in how they "saw" the wolf? Discuss point of view and speaker identification. Why was it so enjoyable to hear this old tale from another perspective?

2. Instruct the students to think about a time they saw or heard about a dog being obedience trained. What kinds of things did the dog have to do? What did the trainer have to do? Write a brief description of this on the board. Next, ask the students to write the description of dog training from the dog's point of view on Figure #25-1, writing in first person as the dog. Share the results with the group.

3. Ask students to re-write a passage from the class novel or reading group book using a different character's point of view. Figure #25-2 outlines how to do this. During the next time the group is reading the novel, ask individuals to share what they have written. This might be an enjoyable activity to act out as a play. Two characters could debate their individual points of view about the plot.

4. Suggest a topic on which you know there are varying viewpoints in the class. Ask students to voice their opinions in a positive, respectful way. Note how this compares to authors using their positions in writing.

5. Bring in newspaper articles, editorials, Internet articles, etc. Ask students to read them and identify the speaker. If you can find multiple articles about the same topic, written by different people with opposing viewpoints, this is an excellent tool for teaching this concept.

A Dog's Point of View

Directions: Imagine you are a puppy. A trainer or your owner is trying to teach you how to obey. He is showing you how to sit, lie down, fetch, and heel. Write about this experience as if you are the dog. What are your feelings? What are you thinking? Describe what is happening. You may draw a picture to go with your story.

Whose Point of View?

Directions: Find a paragraph in your book that you think is interesting. Rewrite this paragraph from another point of view. If it is written from the perspective of a character, try changing which character is telling the story. If it is being told by a narrator or storyteller, write it as if someone in the story is telling it.

Title of book: _____

Write the paragraph from the book.

_____

_____

_____

_____

_____

_____

Write the paragraph from a different point of view (use the back of this paper, if necessary).

_____

_____

_____

_____

_____

_____

_____

_____

Quiz—Point of View

1. What is point of view?

   _____

   _____

2. What is first-person point of view?

   _____

   _____

3. What is third-person point of view?

   _____

   _____

4. Think about the novel you are reading. From whose point of view is the novel written?

   _____

   _____

5. Why is it important for readers to understand point of view?

   _____

   _____

6. Rewrite this poem from Jack's point of view. Use the back of this sheet if necessary.

   Jack and Jill went up the hill
   To fetch a pail of water.
   Jack fell down and broke his crown
   And Jill came tumbling after.

   _____

   _____

   _____

Name: _____

Figure #25-4

Reading Connection Newsletter

Dear Parents/Guardians:

An understanding of point of view is essential to all comprehension. Knowing who is "doing the talking" is important to all readers because we all need to understand the source of the ideas and feelings we find in print. It would be very difficult to understand a novel that is written from the viewpoint of a character if we thought it was being told by an outside narrator. This week we learned about first- and third-person writing. We practiced writing from different points of view and found examples in our reading.

Next week we will be learning about dialogue and how it is used to make reading more interesting. As you document at-home reading on the log below, be sure to ask about point of view. Was the material written in first person (by someone in the story) or third person (by a storyteller or narrator outside the story)? Thank you for your follow-through of skills we are learning at school.

Please write the date next to each day.

Friday _____	Saturday _____	Sunday _____	Monday _____
Minutes read	Minutes read	Minutes read	Minutes read
_____	_____	_____	_____
Tuesday _____	Wednesday _____	Thursday _____	
Minutes read	Minutes read	Minutes read	
_____	_____	_____	

Student's name _____

Parent/Guardian signature _____ Date _____

Week 26—Dialogue

Reading dialogue is an important skill for readers. Understanding the mechanics of quotation marks and speech tags makes reading much easier and comprehension more complete. Additionally, knowing that the direct speech of a character can tell the reader more about that character is also a valuable concept. This leads to improved interpretation and fluency when reading.

Dialogue between characters is important because it: 1. tells the reader much about the character, such as emotions, use of slang, regional dialect, how he/she reacts to what others are saying or doing; and 2. tells about the relationships between characters by the way they communicate with each other.

Lessons and Activities

1. Introduce the concept of dialogue as two or more characters talking to each other. Explain that quotation marks and speech tags are part of dialogue and that the class will practice identifying, working with, and writing dialogue this week. Give examples from the current class novel by initially reading a passage with dialogue. Then ask students to raise and wiggle the index and middle fingers of both hands before and after the direct quotations as you read. Explain that they have just put in quotation marks.

2. Using sentence strips on which you have written sentences containing quotations, ask students to use elbow pasta as quotation marks to be glued onto the strips in the correct position. Even older students like to do a fun activity like this, and it keeps the concept in their minds, appealing especially to the tactile students in the class.

3. Using cartoons from the newspaper, explain that the speech bubbles showing the words of the characters are actually quotations and that the entire comic strip is a good example of dialogue. Ask the students to look at an example on the overhead projector. Tell a story using the actual quotations as written in the bubbles and your own words to complete the story. Pass out other cartoons and Figure #26-1. Ask students to write a story that makes sense with the cartoon and uses the dialogue.

4. Distribute novels or other books with a lot of dialogue. Direct the students to take the roles of the characters. Read the text out loud until you come to quotation marks. Students then read their parts, letting you interject speech tags, if necessary. This activity reinforces the concept of direct quotations being the speakers' exact words.

5. Ask one student each day to prepare a quotation for the class. It might be as simple as "Have a good day." Then, on a special place on the board, write the quotation each day. This might look like, Casey says, "It looks like rain today." This is just one more reminder that speakers' exact words go between quotation marks, and it gives each child the opportunity to feel important and heard.

6. Figure #26-2 requires students to read sentences and place quotation marks where they belong. Other punctuation is already provided to make this an exercise specific to quotation marks.

7. Assign a paper to be written with a minimum of ten examples of dialogue between the characters. You might want to give required characters, problems, etc., to help those who might have a problem getting started with this assignment.

Cartoon Dialogue

Directions: Using the comic strip your teacher has provided, read the dialogue between the characters. Then, fill in the information below. Finally, write a few paragraphs about the cartoon. Be sure to use the exact quotations from the comic strip in your paragraphs.

Name of comic strip: _____

Characters: _____

Setting: _____

What are they talking about? _____

_____

Write the comic strip in the form of a story.

_____

_____

_____

_____

_____

_____

_____

_____

_____

_____

_____

What Did You Say?

Directions: Write quotation marks where they are needed in the following sentences.

1. While walking along the road, Jim said, I am getting hungry.

2. Mary asked, What are the names of the puppies?

3. I think I will invite all my friends to a party, Nancy said, and they will need to bring their bathing suits.

4. Is this the way to the skate park? asked Nate.

5. After taking the test, Lisa said, I think I did very well today.

6. My grandma is coming to visit us next week, said Dave.

7. Susie screamed, I am afraid of dogs!

8. Go to your room right away, young man, Mother said in a loud voice.

9. The child cried softly, I want my mom.

Quiz—Dialogue

1. What is dialogue?

   _____

   _____

   _____

2. When do writers use quotation marks?

   _____

   _____

   _____

3. What are speech tags?

   _____

   _____

   _____

4. What do speech tags tell readers about the speaker?

   _____

   _____

   _____

5. Why is it important to know about dialogue when you are reading?

   _____

   _____

   _____

Name: _____

Figure #26-4

Reading Connection Newsletter

Dear Parents/Guardians:

　　Dialogue between two or more characters makes reading more interesting and gives more meaning to what is being read. Certainly, any novel you have read as an adult has been more enjoyable because of the dialogue. This week we learned to recognize and use dialogue in our reading and writing. We practiced using quotation marks and understanding that they go around a character's exact words. We found quotations in our reading and wrote our own stories with dialogue. This week as we read at home, we should be looking for dialogue. Please help with this during at-home reading time.

　　Next week we will be learning about fixing our comprehension when we can't understand what we are reading.

　　Thank you for all you do to help us become better readers. The practice and encouragement we get at home is reflected in our work at school. Please fill out this week's at-home reading log and send it back next Friday morning.

Please write the date next to each day.

Friday _____	Saturday _____	Sunday _____	Monday _____
Minutes read	Minutes read	Minutes read	Minutes read
_____	_____	_____	_____
Tuesday _____	Wednesday _____	Thursday _____	
Minutes read	Minutes read	Minutes read	
_____	_____	_____	

Student's name _____

Parent/Guardian signature _____ Date _____

Week 27—Fixing Comprehension

Students must learn how to fix the problems they have in understanding what they read. They must be able to do this independently, as there is not always a teacher or other help nearby when they can't comprehend. The first step in learning how to take care of problems is to learn to self-diagnose. The previous sections in this book have all described important comprehension skills and strategies and how to use them. Students should be aware of how they use these skills daily as they read. Therefore, when they are having difficulty, they can easily see what is not working properly. By supplying a list of reminders of these previously-learned strategies, a teacher is giving a valuable resource for help. Posting such a list on the wall of the classroom is useful because it is always there where students can refer to it by themselves.

Ask students what they do when they realize they are not understanding what they are reading. The answers will vary. Some might say:
- I quit reading.
- I re-read everything.
- I break it down into little parts I can understand.
- I ask for help.

What should students do when comprehension is lost? First, they must be aware of what they do know or understand. This can be accomplished by a wall chart of skills and strategies learned so far in class, like the one shown below. Next, they need to identify what they do not understand in the text. What is giving them trouble? What does not make sense? Perhaps they can go back to where they first discovered that they did not comprehend. What happened at that point? Was there unfamiliar vocabulary they skipped? Did the text take an unexpected twist? Find the point where the problems began. Finally, they need to refer to the skills they already have. Looking at the wall chart will give them ideas about what the problem might be and how to fix it.

The chart should include the following steps, and students should ask themselves if they used these strategies.

☆ Make a prediction.

☆ Identify the problem.

☆ Ask for help.

☆ Use graphic organizers to help yourself understand.

☆ Make a connection to yourself, another text, or the world.

☆ Look back and forward to find answers.

☆ Summarize, paraphrase, or retell the material.

☆ Visualize—make a picture or movie in your head.

Lessons and Activities

1. Discuss what the students do when they cannot understand their text. Ask students to write ideas from other students that they find useful. Pass out laminated bookmarks that have the following steps written on them.

1. Identify the problem.

2. Look back or look forward.

3. Visualize by making a mental movie.

4. Summarize or paraphrase.

5. Use graphic organizers.

6. Make a connection.

7. Make a prediction.

8. Ask for help.

Explain that these are steps they can use when comprehension is lost. Discuss each step. Ask the students if these will help. Make clear that problems understanding text happen to all readers. Tell the students to keep the bookmark with their name on it in their current reading material for reference. Keep plenty of replacements for lost bookmarks.

2. Distribute Figure #27-1, asking the students to read the article on the page and think of strategies they would employ to understand the text. This is written at a higher reading level than most material for these grade levels, so explain that this is not to frustrate, only to practice using strategies.

3. Make fixing comprehension a part of every reading assignment for the rest of the school year. Ask, "What could I do if I didn't understand what we just read?" This will give students plenty of opportunities to practice this important work and make it an automatic part of their reading in all classes.

What Does It Mean?

Directions: Read the paragraph on this page. Then write three strategies you could use to understand what you read.

    Although some people think dolphins resemble fish, they are, in fact, mammals. They are streamlined, like fish, which makes their swimming smooth and fast. However, their locomotion is made possible by moving their tail up and down, rather than side to side like a fish. Replacing a fish's fins in the front of the dolphin's body are flippers. A dolphin's skin is smooth, while a fish's skin is scaly.

What strategies can you use to understand this article?

1. _____

   _____

   _____

2. _____

   _____

   _____

3. _____

   _____

   _____

Quiz—Fixing Comprehension

1. Why might you have to fix your comprehension?

_____

_____

_____

_____

_____

2. Name six strategies for fixing comprehension.

   a. _____

   b. _____

   c. _____

   d. _____

   e. _____

   f. _____

3. Which strategy do you use most?

_____

_____

_____

_____

_____

Name: _____

Figure #27-3

Reading Connection Newsletter

Dear Parents/Guardians:

Throughout this year we have been working on strategies to make comprehension of reading material effective and easy. This week we learned how to put all those strategies and skills together to help when we simply cannot understand what we are reading. The steps we talked about using are:

1. Identify the problem.
2. Look back and forward in the text to find answers.
3. Visualize by making a mental movie.
4. Summarize or paraphrase.
5. Use graphic organizers.
6. Make a connection with self, other text, or the world.
7. Make a prediction.
8. Ask for help.

We have these steps listed on a bookmark to use at school. Making one for home might be a good idea, too.

Next week we will be talking about reading enjoyment and good books.

Please fill out the at-home reading form at the bottom of this page and return it to school next Friday morning. Thank you.

Please write the date next to each day.

Friday _____	Saturday _____	Sunday _____	Monday _____
Minutes read	Minutes read	Minutes read	Minutes read
_____	_____	_____	_____
Tuesday _____	Wednesday _____	Thursday _____	
Minutes read	Minutes read	Minutes read	
_____	_____	_____	

Student's name _____

Parent/Guardian signature _____ Date _____

Week 28—Reading Enjoyment

Reading teachers often realize that they are doing more than just teaching skills. They are preparing students to succeed in almost every aspect of their lives. Reading puts in order all the tasks that involve print and text of any kind throughout life. There is something just as important that teachers can impart to their students through their literacy studies: love of reading. What a tragedy it would be to turn out students who can read fluently, but have never enjoyed reading. Well-informed, well-trained readers enjoy experiencing the joy of good books, the delight of meeting and knowing characters, and visiting exotic places through literature. When students approach their teacher and say, "This is the best book I have ever read. Let me tell you about it," the teacher knows that success is at hand. The student has learned that reading is a source of pleasure. The job of teaching has its reward.

"I used to hate reading. Now I really like it," coming from a student is music to a teacher's ears. "I can't get his head out of a book," coming from a parent makes the work of developing readers worthwhile. Providing high-interest, level-appropriate materials in abundance in the reading classroom for self-selection by students is the first step in making these success stories reality.

Lessons and Activities

1. Book Shares were mentioned earlier in this book. If possible, weekly shares should take place. Students truly enjoy hearing each other talk about interesting books. What a great way to develop lists of books to be read! "Jackie loved this book. I might like it too," is much more powerful than a teacher, librarian, or parent recommendation. Arranging the classroom in a different configuration for this activity is a good idea. It is a signal that something special is about to happen. Make sure each child is able to see and hear everyone else. Provide snacks, if you like, to make this extra-special. Each student should also have paper and pencil to write down the titles of books that sound interesting.

2. Have students complete Figure #28-1. This form asks students to become more aware of their preferences in reading material and can be used at any time during the year.

3. Have students complete Figure #28-2 using the current class novel to discover more ways to make reading enjoyable.

4. If students have favorite authors, they can write letters to them. Sometimes an address is hard to find, so send the letters directly to the publishing company that produces that author's work. Authors are very good about answering letters from children, and this is a satisfying experience for students.

5. Remember to always allow plenty of time to look through the classroom library. This can be an activity to do when all work has been finished or a regularly-scheduled center activity. Scheduling trips to the Media Center or the community's public library are also ways to expose students to more literature. Make sure that everyone in the class has that all-important library card!

6. There is not a quiz for this chapter. This work is ongoing and should be revisited regularly.

What I Like to Read

Directions: Answer the following questions to find out more about what kinds of books you like to read. Use these answers to help you choose books in the library or bookstore.

1. What is the best book you have ever read? _____

   _____

2. Have you ever read a book more than once? Which one? Why? _____

   _____

3. Do you have a favorite author? Who is it? Why? _____

   _____

   _____

4. What genre of book do you like best (mysteries, adventure, humor, etc.)?

   _____

5. Have you ever read a book you didn't like? What was it? Why? _____

   _____

   _____

6. If you could talk to an author and tell them what to write about, what would you say?

   _____

   _____

   _____

Questions about Books

Directions: Sometimes you may not enjoy a book assigned by your teacher. Use the questions below as you read and see if the book is more interesting to read.

1. Are there illustrations in the book? What are they like?

2. Is the book organized in an easy-to-read format?

3. Are the characters interesting?

4. Can you make any personal connections with the characters?

5. Are you making predictions as you read?

6. Are you visualizing the text?

7. Are you asking questions in your head as you read?

8. Could you write a play or skit about this book?

9. Can you draw a picture as you read?

10. Can you make up test questions about the book as you read?

Now tell how you used one of these questions during your reading. Did it make the book more interesting?

_____

_____

_____

_____

Name: _____

Figure #28-3

Reading Connection Newsletter

Dear Parents/Guardians:

This week we discussed reading for enjoyment. We shared books that we each really liked and got ideas from each other for books we might want to read someday. We learned that there are ways to make reading even textbooks enjoyable, if we just use some strategies like making predictions and visualizing. There is so much more to reading than skills. People who love to read are never bored because there are always exciting adventures to be had in books. This year of reading discovery is only the beginning of a lifetime of reading. Please model the enjoyment of reading and share books with your child.

Please fill out the at-home reading log below and return it to school next Friday. Thank you.

Please write the date next to each day.

Friday _____ Minutes read _____	Saturday _____ Minutes read _____	Sunday _____ Minutes read _____	Monday _____ Minutes read _____
Tuesday _____ Minutes read _____	Wednesday _____ Minutes read _____	Thursday _____ Minutes read _____	

Student's name _____

Parent/Guardian signature _____ Date _____

Appendix I—Suggested Class Novels

The following lists are arranged in grade-level categories. These are flexible, but do contain excellent examples of the literature available for grade 3–5 students. The final list is designated "mixed" and contains text at a relatively easy reading level with the possibility of being of interest to all students in these grade levels. Teachers can use any of the books at any grade level, as they see fit for the unique characteristics of each class.

Grade 3

The Beast in Ms. Rooney's Room—Patricia Reilly Giff
The Candy Corn Contest—Patricia Reilly Giff
Cloudy with a Chance of Meatballs—Judi Barrett
*Encyclopedia Brown series—Donald J. Sobol
*Freckle Juice—Judy Blume
The Giving Tree—Shel Silverstein
Humphrey the Wayward Whale—Ernest Callenbach
*The Indian in the Cupboard—Lynne Reid Banks
*Ira Sleeps Over—Bernard Waber
Knots on a Counting Rope—John Archambault
Mufaro's Beautiful Daughter—John Steptoe
*Nate the Great series—Marjorie Sharmat
*Ramona Quimby, Age 8—Beverly Cleary
*Stone Fox—John Reynolds Gardiner
*Tales of a Fourth Grade Nothing—Judy Blume
The True Story of the Three Little Pigs—Jon Scieszka

Grade 4

*Anastasia Krupnik—Lois Lowry
*Because of Winn-Dixie—Kate DiCamillo
*Bunnicula—James Howe
*Chocolate Touch—Patrick Skene Catling
Fudge-a-Mania—Judy Blume
The Gold Cadillac—Mildred D. Taylor
The Good, the Bad and the Goofy—Jon Scieszka
*How to Eat Fried Worms—Thomas Rockwell
*James and the Giant Peach—Roald Dahl
*The Lion, the Witch and the Wardrobe—C.S. Lewis
Love that Dog—Sharon Creech
Otherwise Known as Sheila the Great—Judy Blume
*Superfudge—Judy Blume
*There's a Boy in the Girls' Bathroom—Louis Sachar
*The Tiger Rising—Kate DiCamillo

Grade 5

*The Borrowers—Mary Norton
*Bridge to Terabithia—Katerine Paterson
The Case of the Elevator Duck—Polly Berrien Berends
Celery Stalks at Midnight—James Howe
*The Cricket in Times Square—George Selden
*Dear Mr. Henshaw—Beverly Cleary
Do Bananas Chew Gum?—Jamie Gilson
A Family Apart—Joan Lowery Nixon
Harris and Me—Gary Paulsen
*Harry Potter series—J.K. Rowling
House on Hackman's Hill—Joan Lowery Nixon
Journey to Topaz—Yoshiko Uchida
*Number the Stars—Lois Lowry
*My Side of the Mountain—Jean Craighead George
*The Pinballs—Betsy Byars
*Tuck Everlasting—Natalie Babbitt
Wayside School Gets a Little Stranger—Louis Sachar
*Wringer—Jerry Spinelli

Mixed Grade Levels

Cam Jansen—David A. Adler
*Charlotte's Web—E.B. White
*Harriet the Spy—Louise Fitzhugh
*Mrs. Frisby and the Rats of NIMH—Robert O'Brien
Paddle to the Sea—Holling C. Holling
*Pippi Longstocking—Astrid Lindgren
Three Perfect Peaches—Cynthia C. Defelice

* Teacher and/or Student Guide available for this title. See novelunits.com for more information.

Appendix II—Bell-starter Activities

As referred to in Week 1, bell-starter, or warm-up, activities focus students on work as soon as they enter the room. These daily class-starters allow the teacher time to greet students at the door, take roll, and attend to the variety of beginning-of-the-day chores that must be accomplished. Bell-starters should have a purpose for students: either to review prior work, prepare for the current day's work, or set a mood of enjoyment to start the day. The bell-starters can be written on the board, and students should work on these assignments until the teacher is ready to begin instruction. Discussion of the bell-starters should last no more than 2–3 minutes.

Bell-starters might include:
1. Riddles
2. Review of the previous day's work
3. Pre-test questions about the current day's work
4. "Mind-bender" problems
5. Surveys
6. "Quick write" assignments
7. Math word problems

Examples of bell-starters:
Mind-benders
1. Which does not belong: apple, banana, cherry, plum? (banana, because you must peel it to eat it)
2. How far can a deer run into the woods? (halfway, after that he's running out of the woods)
3. You are driving a bus. At the first stop 3 people get on. At the second stop 1 person gets off and 4 get on. At the third stop 6 people get on and 5 get off. What color are the bus driver's eyes? (You are the bus driver!)

Riddles
1. What's black and white and red all over? (a blushing zebra)
2. What did one wall say to the other wall? (Meet you at the corner.)
3. Which side of a cat has the most fur? (the outside)
4. What is 5 F on an H? (fingers on a hand)
5. What is 50 S on an F? (stars on a flag)

Surveys
1. Name your five favorite ice cream flavors.
2. List three places you'd like to visit.
3. Name your five favorite pizza toppings.
4. Name your four best friends.
5. What is the nicest sound you've ever heard?

 ⋯ *POWer Strategies™ for Reading Comprehension Grades 3–5*